The Contemplative Hunger

FR. DONALD HAGGERTY

The Contemplative Hunger

IGNATIUS PRESS   SAN FRANCISCO

Cover photograph by Tom Pfeiffer

Sunrise over salt lake Assale, Ethiopia

Cover design by Roxanne Mei Lum

© 2016 by Ignatius Press, San Francisco
All rights reserved
ISBN 978-1-62164-033-2
Library of Congress Control Number 2015939072
Printed in the United States of America ∞

To

Sister M. Nirmala, M.C. (1934–2015)

and

Sister M. Priscilla, M.C. (1934–2011)

Contents

Foreword 9

Introduction 15

1. A Contemplative Revolution? 21

2. Thorn and Goad: The Loss of Religious
   Truth 35

3. Contemplative Intimations 53

4. The Contemplative and the Poor 67

5. Contemplative Kinship with Poverty . . . 83

6. Affinity for the Full Gift of Self 99

7. The Import of Contemplative
   Surrenders 115

8. The Allure of Silence 133

9. Interior Deportment in Prayer 149

10. Notes on Contemplative Prayer 167

11. Bedrock Faith and Contemplation . . . 189

12. Contemplative Hurdles and Stumbling
    Blocks 207

13. Contemplative Aftereffects 227

14. Observations in Brief 243

Foreword

In his Apostolic Letter *Novo Millennio Ineunte*, Pope Saint John Paul II expressed the particular task of the Church in our time: a new evangelization. In describing the call to a new evangelization, that is, to living and proclaiming the Catholic Faith with the enthusiasm and the energy of the first disciples, the saintly Pontiff reflected that we will not save ourselves and our world by discovering "some magic formula" or by "inventing a new program". In unmistakable terms, he declared:

No, we shall not be saved by a formula but by a Person, and the assurance which he gives us: *I am with you.*

He reminded us that the program by which we are to address effectively the great spiritual challenges of our time is, in the end, Jesus Christ alive for us in the Church.

Urging us to take up a new evangelization, Pope John Paul II explained carefully the way:

The program already exists: it is the plan found in the Gospel and in the living Tradition, it is the same as ever. Ultimately, it has its center in Christ himself, who is to be known, loved and imitated, so that in him we may live the life of the Trinity, and with him transform history until its fulfillment in the heavenly Jerusalem.

Our Lord Himself is the Way, as He teaches us: "I am the way, and the truth, and the life; no one comes to the Father, but by me."

The program of the New Evangelization, then, is "starting afresh from Christ". This begins with "contemplation of the face of Christ" in prayer. Saint John Paul II stated:

> It is important . . . that what we propose, with the help of God, should be profoundly rooted in contemplation and prayer. Ours is a time of continual movement which often leads to restlessness, with the risk of "doing for the sake of doing". We must resist this temptation by trying "to be" before trying "to do".

Our Lord Himself is our example in His frequent retreats to the mountain or to a place apart, in order to be alone with the Father in prayer, for example, before beginning His public ministry and before entering into His Passion. He taught the Apostles to do the same.

In *The Contemplative Hunger*, Father Donald Haggerty has provided a wealth of reflections for all those who seek to contemplate the face of Christ.

His reflections describe vividly the experience of a soul which seeks God in prayer, and which, amidst darkness and trials, perseveres in giving itself to God with the pure and selfless love that flows unceasingly and immeasurably from the Heart of Jesus into Christian souls. Father Haggerty reminds us that God desires to give Himself to each of us, a gift which is given most perfectly in the Holy Eucharist. God's longing to give Himself to us should provoke, in turn, a hunger in our souls for union with God. Father Haggerty vividly portrays this hunger, as well as the obstacles that it encounters in our world and the means by which it can be cultivated and the obstacles can be overcome.

In fact, the hunger for God is constantly opposed in today's society, which has become so completely secularized that many live "as if God did not exist". Father Haggerty explains the challenge that this presents to living a contemplative life, since today's society presents an unprecedented number of distractions which can blunt the hunger for God. At the same time, he points out that, precisely as a response to the secularism of our time, the grace of God seems to be drawing many Christians, in the midst of the world, to a deeper life of contemplation, marked particularly by adoration of Our Lord in the Blessed Sacrament.

Father Haggerty's reflections on the contemplative life are rooted firmly in Catholic doctrine.

In contrast with certain confused notions which would equate Christian contemplation with the methods of meditation practiced in other world religions, Father Haggerty recognizes that the gift of self to God which occurs in contemplative prayer requires the docility of our intellect to the truths of faith revealed by God and taught in the Church's doctrine. Doctrine is not a hindrance to a personal relationship with Our Lord in prayer but, rather, an indispensable precondition of that salvific relationship.

Furthermore, he shows how the contemplative encounter with the infinite mystery of God is only possible through the encounter with Jesus Christ, God the Son Incarnate, particularly in His Eucharistic Presence. Participation in the Eucharistic Sacrifice and communion in its incomparable fruit, the Body, Blood, Soul and Divinity of Christ, is the highest and most perfect expression of our contemplation and prayer. Father Haggerty's reflections thus contribute to rekindling the "Eucharistic amazement" which Saint John Paul II wished for the whole Church.

Drawing on his own wealth of experience in serving the poor, Father Haggerty also describes the intimate connection between the love of God in contemplative prayer and the love of our neighbor without limit or boundary. A true encounter with God in contemplation, in fact, always leads to a fuller gift of self in pure and selfless love to our brothers and sisters, especially those in most need. The contemplation of the face of Christ in prayer draws us in turn to contemplate and give ourselves to Christ Whom we encounter in the poorest of the poor.

The path of the contemplative life, as described by Father Haggerty, is an arduous one. In fact, it is a path which can only be walked by the abandonment of ourselves to God in childlike confidence. It is not by chance that the first of the Beatitudes, the heart of the Sermon on the Mount, is: "Blessed are the poor in spirit, for theirs is the kingdom of heaven." Father Haggerty's description of the "poverty" experienced by souls on the path of the contemplative life naturally brings to mind the teaching of Saint Thérèse of the Child Jesus on the "Little Way" of spiritual childhood. This Little Way, which is in fact the way of all contemplative souls, is based on the humility which recognizes our nothingness before God. Far from leading to discouragement, this humility leads to a total confidence in God our Father, and thence to a total abandonment of self to His love, as Our Lord Himself assures us in the teaching of the Beatitudes. Abandoning ourselves more and more to the merciful love of God, our poor and sinful hearts are transformed by the Sacred Heart of Jesus, so that, by the work of His grace, they reflect ever more perfectly His pure and selfless love of God and of all men.

It is my fervent hope that Father Haggerty's reflections will assist many to "put out into the deep" of the life of prayer, so as to be transformed by contemplating the Face of Christ, and thus to become fervent apostles of a new evangelization in our time and place. May the Blessed Virgin Mary, who is both the model of contemplative souls and the Star of the New Evangelization, obtain for all who read these reflections the grace to share in her contemplation of the Face of Christ, and to be ever more perfect instruments of His truth and love to the people of our time and our place.

Raymond Leo Cardinal Burke
November 1, 2015
Solemnity of All Saints

Introduction

"If, then, I am no longer seen or found on the common, you will say that I am lost; but stricken by love, I lost myself, and was found."

—Saint John of the Cross

A hunger for God, once it seizes our soul, does not disappear easily, and for that we must be grateful to God. Indeed, we can assume that he will continue to intensify this hunger if only we respond to it. All that is needed initially may be a discovery that God is offering himself to us in a very personal manner. It can be that we often understand spiritual pursuit primarily as our dutiful submission to God's call and command. The response of faithfulness is undoubtedly important, but there is another truth to which we do not pay sufficient attention. This truth is that God wants to give himself to our soul, a truth abundantly clear in the great sacramental reality of the Holy Eucharist. The same truth is also the basis for the contemplative life of greater intimacy and encounter with God. The discovery of

God in any profound sense provokes a hunger in our soul to experience him more personally.

Charles de Foucauld famously recorded his own sense of this hunger for God after the recovery of his Catholic faith. "The moment I knew that God existed, I realized that I could do nothing but live for him alone." These are words of a saint in the making. But in a parallel manner, they are an apt description for the piercing hunger for God that seizes the heart of every contemplative soul. The experience of that hunger ordinarily incites a quest for God in the adventure of deeper prayer. Prayer truly begins to capture our longing the moment we realize that Our Lord is offering himself to us and that our heart wants nothing more than this. Then we must set out, never tiring of the quest for God. We can be quite sure that he awaits us in this journey of prayer. He will meet us, and he will also hide from us, but he will never allow our hunger to leave us as long as we keep returning to prayer.

Too easily, perhaps, we consider the life of contemplative prayer to be restricted to a special vocation in itself. In this limited view, anyone who remains in the world cannot possibly aspire to a deeper contemplative encounter with God. But this is clearly a wrong notion. A discipline and a commitment to prayer are required, an effort of much self-giving, more than we may have lived yet, but certainly a deeper life of prayer is open to every soul. God surely wants this inasmuch as he desires love from us and union with us. It is not necessary to examine our qualifications or suitability. A short statement of the Carthusian Augustin Guillerand can be understood precisely as an invitation to a more intense life of prayer for those living in the world, not simply for a monk:

> God is the soul of our soul: that is the source that gives it life. It is there that we must seek Him, and it is there we shall find Him without end. That is what the saints did. They kept themselves before the face of the living God. And God, thus contemplated by an interior regard, communicated Himself to them and lived in them. . . . It can be so with us, even in our busiest moments. It is not necessary to seek the stillness of a sanctuary. All we need to do is to make an act of faith and of love: "My God, I believe in you, and I love you." A simple movement in the depths of our soul that we call forth from time to time.

Certainly these words are meant for all and fitting for all who aspire to deeper relations with God. We have only to recognize what our own soul at its depth may be begging us to perceive.

The present collection of spiritual thoughts is a complementary work and sequel to the earlier *Contemplative Provocations* (2013). It is written in a similar style as the previous book—concise and concentrated observations that can stimulate some personal reflection from the reader on serious points of prayer and spiritual life. Much of the underlying motive behind the earlier work was to impart attraction for the life of prayer and for the adventure of a wholehearted pursuit of God. The same is true here. In the earlier book, the concealment of God from the soul who seeks him with greater fervor was a thematic undercurrent in the reflections. The hiddenness of God for the soul who loves him is indeed a great provocation to contemplative life. The experience of this hiddenness of God draws a soul more intently to the full gift of self and to deeper prayer.

The effort in this book is to turn to another challenge that likewise animates all contemplative life. In this case, the challenge comes from a graced source within our own soul. This is the truth of the hunger of soul that takes possession of all contemplative souls and does not release them. That challenge calls as well for certain recognitions and a significant generosity. At the same time, no soul who seeks God in earnest considers it burdensome to plunge more deeply in an offering of itself to God. The discovery of God's desire for the complete gift and surrender of our soul is, on the contrary, a great incentive to prayer and self-offering. The awareness of this spiritual demand as "the one thing necessary" does not leave our soul once we begin to offer ourselves more fully to God. A contemplative soul would not want it otherwise and happily accedes to this demand of love.

Admittedly, then, the motive behind this work is a transparent desire to draw souls to prayer. My own experience in the priesthood is that those who are more serious about prayer are invariably greater in their fruitfulness for the good of souls. This obvious remark is nonetheless not enough to bring people to the commitment of prayer. That choice has to be undertaken in a very personal manner. Yet who has ever regretted a commitment to seek God in a more concentrated manner? Our souls have been created for the personal encounter with God in prayer while we live in this life. We have only to respond to the hunger that is present within us to begin savoring this love for prayer. Those, on the other hand, who think that prayer impedes a life of active generosity or is simply incompatible with a busy life in the world are mistaken. On given days we may not find the time we desire for prayer. But souls who hunger for God in a deeply personal way are not denied what their soul longs for, and God seems to make sure of this. Moreover, everyone who is serious in the pursuit of prayer seems always to possess a more intense spiritual energy for the active demands of life. The saints to this day are a vivid testimony of this truth.

One last remark might be made. The struggle

in the spiritual realm between faith and the loss of religious belief is an increasingly pronounced reality in contemporary life. The initial chapters of this book are an effort to expose some aspects and implications of the struggle that religious faith is facing today. Contemplative life cannot ignore them: indeed, it must thrust itself into the heart of this tension. The serious commitment to the life of deeper prayer may be the only response that can adequately oppose the dismissal of God from human lives. The presence of prayer in our lives is an enormous counterweight to the growing tendency to disbelief. But we must experience this for ourselves. A hidden strength and influence are imparted to our soul when we take prayer seriously. Above all, there is a great need for priests and religious to return to the importance of prayer. Their lives, if deeply prayerful, cannot but have an impact on the faith of others. But it ought to be said as well that prayerful lay people are showing perhaps even more than priests and religious that a spiritual flame rooted in prayer extends its influence into the world in the most inconspicuous and yet profound ways. These prayerful souls among lay people are in fact a current marvel in the Church. In some cases, they are the young fathers and mothers who will raise children to be the next generation of priests and religious.

I

A Contemplative Revolution?

"The mystical capacity of the human mind needs to be strengthened again. The capacity to renounce oneself, a greater inner openness, the discipline to withdraw ourselves from noise and from all that presses on our attention, should once more be for all of us goals that we recognize as being among our priorities."

—Joseph Ratzinger

"There is but one road which reaches God, and that is prayer; if anyone shows you another, you are being deceived."

—Saint Teresa of Avila

"With contemplation, we shall do more for ourselves and others in a month than we shall do without it in ten years."

—Père Lallemant, S.J.

Contemplative life is a mystery of grace. It is a response to a profound attraction to God drawing a soul to seek God in prayer. For many lives, it is the great love of their life to carve out reserved time for God in daily silent prayer.

At the same time, contemplative life is never a personal pursuit alone. It has always a relationship with the larger struggle of Christian belief in the contemporary world. The evidence is strong today that a desire for silent prayer is being felt by more and more souls, a phenomenon most notable for taking place outside cloisters and monasteries. It is a spiritual sign of the times. This leaning in attraction toward more intensive prayer within the Church may reflect a reaction to the growing indifference to God in the larger world. Perhaps only those who commit themselves more fully to prayer can realize the connection. The quiet hunger for deeper prayer may in fact be the most vital deterrent to the increasing tide of secularization in the current world.

Can a "contemplative revolution" take place in the Church? A significant turn among many souls to the fundamental importance of silent prayer in hours alone before the gaze of God? Surely spiritual upheavals do happen at certain periods in the Church's history. But in this case it would primarily mean a concealed action undertaken by large numbers of hidden souls in quiet corners of the Church, yet fruitful in ways that cannot be evaluated so easily. Unlike reforms that are more public and visible, this one is unlikely to show dramatic effects or influences so immediate. The repercussions of contemplative life occur in the mysterious realm of hidden graces and usually take time.

Nonetheless, the contemplative lives in any era are a great flame burning beneath the endeavors of the Church. This influence does not just come from the contemplatives praying in cloisters and monasteries. Souls of contemplation who give themselves in apostolic works plant seeds of spiritual hunger in many souls around them. An encounter with them is often the beginning of a profound need to find God personally in a love for prayer.

∼

Not every historical period in the Church displays the same tendencies toward a radical gift of the soul to God. Ordinarily, we see this radicality in the spiritual life in visible ways. Sometimes, however, the testimony of spiritual intensity may be most evident in the concealed heroism of contemplative paths. There might be a reason for this latter tendency. It may be that Christianity in those times is not so distinguished from a contemporary culture. The preference for some commitment to a contemplative solitude may reflect the difficulty that souls encounter in a time of compromised faith. This choice for what can seem to some extent a solitary path to God may give the appearance of a withdrawal from the primary importance of evangelical witness in the Church, which remains always a perennial need. It is nonetheless true that spiritually intense souls are often unable to abide comfortably in religious environments of compromise and relative spiritual apathy. We might ask whether this phenomenon is true today. Cloisters and monasteries show no noticeable influx of candidates. On the other hand, solitary souls of spiritual intensity seem to be increasing all the time. By this is meant, not an eccentric option for isolation from others, but a deeper tendency among some people to hunger for solitary prayer and time alone with God. Souls of intense yearning for God seem to be making their influence felt more and more in the Church today, and precisely because they are often souls who make a greater contribution to active works as well. These people seem to be finding their way to God and to hours of silent prayer even in places that are less congenial for deeper spiritual living. They are a spiritual phenomenon of the current day in the Church.

∼

There are paradigm shifts in the history of spirituality as there are in the history of science or law or technology. These are major innovations at certain periods in the radical pursuit of God. Options in spirituality that earlier did not exist suddenly become possible, attracting a contagious, expansive response. These transitions occur precisely when a

hunger for God intensifies without a correspond-
ing opportunity present in the current structures
of spirituality for satiating it. Assuaging that deeper
yearning for God demands something more radical. The innovation then arrives as a supernatural response to the desire for a more radical offering to God. A classic ancient example of such a
paradigm shift occurred with the influx of many
thousands of men, and women as well, into the
extreme harshness of solitary life in the Egyptian
and Syrian deserts after the Roman martyrdoms
ceased in the early fourth century. The innovation
of mendicant life in the medieval period is another
example, again drawing thousands, in reaction to
the uninspiring comforts besetting monastic and
clerical life at that time. The early Jesuit revolution,
after the start of the Protestant Reformation, calling men to go forth into the streets of Europe and
to far-flung missions and heroic martyrdoms is another instance of this contagious appeal for a radical
spiritual choice. In more recent times, a paradigm
shift in missionary life can perhaps be noted in
Mother Teresa's order, adopting a missionary life
of touching the wounds of Christ in the most desperate lives of the poorest of the poor. The question now is whether another paradigm shift in spirituality is taking place—in this case, a more quiet
and inconspicuous one, yet quite real nonetheless.
A yearning for more prayer and for deeper prayer

seems to be spreading among laity as well as among priests and religious. A contemplative movement of spiritually linked souls, joined invisibly in many cases by a love for the silent prayer of Eucharistic adoration, may be somewhat hidden by its nature and go unnoticed and yet be a leaven of much grace and conversion throughout the Church in this new century.

~

Certainly since the time of Charles de Foucauld and his contemplative life of shared poverty among nomadic Muslim tribesmen in the deserts of North Africa, the missionary life in the Church has acquired a new model. His was a lived presence of poverty and prayer among non-Christian people rather than an explicit effort to add to a measurable count of newly baptized Christians. In fact, he converted no Muslims, to his own disappointment, before suffering martyrdom in Algeria in 1916. The idea of missionary life in this manner implies the paradox of the "uselessness" of a largely hidden life without an opportunity to influence great numbers. But the further question may be asked of whether this model of spirituality is not just an isolated and alternative approach in an inhospitable missionary location or whether it is, rather, a particular sign of the times in which the Church now lives. The quiet witness of contemplative presence and a solidarity in poverty with those who are poor may be the most essential holiness the Church needs today.

～

Contemplative life cannot prosper in detachment from the contemporary crisis in belief. It would betray itself by disappearing behind walls, retreating into the breezes and shades of a garden enclosure. True contemplative life accepts, instead, a confrontation with the surging tendency toward unbelief in our own day. Even in the protected setting of a cloister or monastery, it must face the necessity of this struggle. A particular monastic life may not do face-to-face battle with opponents of religious faith. But if contemplative life is entered into fully, it involves a strain and struggle over a lifetime to cross thresholds of constantly deeper faith. And in this manner, it opposes unbelief and certainly achieves unseen victories. Without realizing, perhaps, the heroic implication of deeper faith, the true contemplative lives in defiance of all efforts to destroy religious faith. Day-to-day perseverance in what may be an obscure and dark faith is always a triumph over the dismissal of faith that seems to gain increasing ground in the current time. It is quite possible in the mystery of God's mercy that the divine graces overflowing from contemplative lives seek out primarily the spiritually lost and the unbelieving as their main target. And this divine action of grace may be effective in a unique way today especially because of contemplative souls who remain living and working in the world.

~

What is the peculiar and dominant approach to God that characterizes our own Western culture and our period of history? What ways of thinking control and set limits to the idea of God in our own time? No easy generalities are really available. But it is possible to make some inferences. Certainly an aversion to transcendent truth is an encrusted attitude among secular intellectuals. A hard, stiffened stance of renunciation prevails toward the transcendent realm of the spiritual. In educated circles, the transcendent is simply an unreal category and ignored. The rejection of the invisible realm of spirit rules and even tyrannizes the culture of secular sophistication. The existence of an immortal human soul is treated with a condescending lack of interest. Only empirical realities are trustworthy claims. These are common observations. But what is not heard is the question of how these intellectual tendencies may affect contemplative life in our time. In fact, the denigration of transcendent truth ought to inflame the desire for contemplation to a greater extent. The intensity of contemplative life in any period ought to find a provocation in the cold repudiation of religious truth. The need to engage and experience the ultimate religious truths known in faith ought to intensify when the surrounding culture scorns traditional religion. But this contemplative response will be necessarily a hidden phenomenon, outside the public eye, and not ordinarily in a direct clash with its adversary.

∼

Contemplative life, even in its concealed quality, may be the most powerful adversary to the tides of secularization undermining religious belief in the modern time. Yet few people even of a serious religious temperament realize this. The ordinary response in the struggle with unbelief is to battle against it with argumentation and visible witness, taking up arms in the public forum. We expect, for instance, strong opposition from leaders in the Church to the secular disregard for moral values. But it may be that the invisible effect of a great turning to God in a personal life of prayer is the strongest antidote against the secular disparagement of Christian faith. This faithfulness to prayer is a witness of a higher order. It is largely unseen by other eyes, yet its influence is active in the realm of spiritual warfare. In that sense, the hidden quality emanating from deeply prayerful lives is only partially concealed. These lives inevitably overflow from their prayer and release a spiritual energy of integrity and a defense of truth into the world.

~

If a crisis of faith continues to afflict Christianity, this will not be primarily an intellectual difficulty with the dogmatic pronouncements of the Catholic faith. Admittedly, the tensions are sharp today between faith's invisible certainties and the secular mentality that would deny reality to the unseen affirmations of faith. But to say that faith is more troublesome for the intellect today than in the past would suggest that human intelligence has diminished with the centuries. The problem is not in understanding the revealed truths proposed by Christianity. These truths of faith have always entailed mysteries that require going beyond ordinary ways of knowledge. And these same mysteries have nonetheless always drawn certain souls of immense intelligence to faith, precisely because a hunger for God burns within the human soul. The real difficulty today in accepting faith is a fierce blunting of a hunger for God. In many people, the human spirit seems almost drained of a deeper need to explore religious questions. The overwhelming availability of distraction has created a kind of barrier of obtuseness to spiritual questions. The consequence of this trend is unknown, inasmuch as it is a truly modern phenomenon. But the tendency raises serious questions about whether, with all the technological thrust of modern life and the loss of a sense of sacred truths, we are heading for a historically significant time of disaster.

～

The absence of spiritual searching is certainly observable in young people. In the contagious behavior that affects youth, many young people seem to live hours each day that are almost programmatically reduced to shallow, impulsive dependencies on visual stimulation and technological chatter. The search for meaning or ultimate truth, once a staple of mature development, has shifted to a compulsive quest for perpetual distraction and the latest text message. All over the world, preoccupied eyes trained downward in a concentrated gaze on a gadget gripped in hand have become an emblematic sign of the times. It can seem almost abnormal for any possibility of spontaneously lifting the mind and heart to God in prayer to interrupt that monopolized focus.

~

The failure to seek truth in the religious realm does not destroy the desire for truth in the soul, which is a natural hunger within our intelligence. This natural yearning for truth will simply turn to less worthy satisfactions. A pragmatic approach to truth will replace a search for more profound transcendent meanings. We ought to be attentive to this danger in our own time. The computer age is made to order for a shift in the natural quest to know truth. The exclusive search for useful information and advantageous knowledge can now consume intelligence. In the narrowing of intelligence to a quest for utilizable truth, an egoism almost inevitably begins to dominate a person's relation to reality. The mind's natural hunger to seek what is true is reduced to a pursuit of knowledge that can serve self. The technological seduction of rapid access to utilitarian knowledge intensifies the illusion of constant gains in all this. But it should be acknowledged that a tragic loss is taking place. The spiritual need for ultimate religious truth is being radically starved. The question of what happens over time as this deeper need for God is unmet has yet to be answered. Surely a form of spiritual nihilism is overtaking societies as we leave unexamined the deeper hungers of the soul for

God and spiritual life. And nihilism has always proven sooner or later to yield a dire and destructive impact.

～

On the other hand, there are souls in every time who yearn for some experience of the invisible realm of the transcendent. Perhaps they have not yet experienced an encounter with the God who draws them to this aspiration. It is important that such souls find their way to faith and Christian prayer. For them it is the only path to a deeper personal happiness in this life. Their great longing can be answered, but only if they discover the beauty of prayer. They will learn in prayer the happiness of a form of touch that the senses cannot reach. Instead of experiencing the transcendent in a tangible way, which may be their initial hope, they will discover in Christian faith the presence of someone who is beyond their senses and never touched and yet is unquestionably real. They will find in faith that there is a way to cleave to God by a profound surrender to him. Then their aspiration to touch the transcendent will flourish even as it remains impossibly beyond an ultimate realization in this life.

～

The simple truth is that the human soul can flourish spiritually only by cultivating a contemplative quality. A commitment to some external quiet in a day is therefore essential. The amount of time may be a personal choice, but the need is undeniable. There may be people who consider this need for silence an eccentric or unnatural impulse. Indeed, it is a regrettable feature of modern life and its technological dependencies that for many people a choice for silence can be completely absent in a typical day. Yet it is only silence that replenishes our inner spirit and keeps a deeper layer of soul in us open to truth. The reason for this is quickly experienced. The presence of some silence in our day has the effect of drawing us to a more generous attentiveness. Silence does not just make us listen better. Its greater impact is on the quality of our eyes. A more selfless act of attention permeates our perception of reality as we live a day. Perhaps we are attracted then to a silence that resides at the heart of all reality and all events. Noise and turmoil may be inescapable, but the surface turbulence is not everything, and a love for silence conveys a deeper truth. It allows us to sense that God is present with his secret gaze upon all that occurs in every day.

2

Thorn and Goad:
The Loss of Religious Truth

"Truth is so obscured in these days and falsehood
so entrenched that unless one loves the truth one
cannot recognize it."
— Blaise Pascal

"The greatest menace to our capacity for contemplation is the incessant fabrication of tawdry,
empty stimuli which kill the receptivity of the
soul."
— Josef Pieper

"What if, beneath all this revelry and group cheer,
there were something seething under our feet?"

— Paul Claudel

*Contemplative life cannot ignore indifference to God and
to religious truth in any current time. Even a cloister or
a monastery is no barrier against the painful recognition
that God can be rejected. Indeed, the hunger for God that
animates the soul of the true contemplative is a cause for a*

more acute suffering in the face of non-belief. The contem-
plative who remains in the world will experience this even
more strongly. Despite some signs today of a resurgence in
Christian faith, it would seem that the crisis of faith in the
contemporary world still deepens. This crisis is inseparable
from a crisis in the understanding of truth. The dissipa-
tion of the human desire to seek ultimate spiritual truths
continues to advance. Awareness of the spiritual tension
between faith and unbelief can be as such a sharp provo-
cation to engage ourselves in a deeper life of prayer. Ne-
glecting prayer, by contrast, is to permit the disappearance
of God to affect more souls over time.

The early morning exchange between Jesus and
Pilate in the praetorium is a perverse epiphany of
all history. It takes the form of an interrogation—
the Son of God on trial and facing a death sentence
before the Roman governor, who has the power to
order Jesus' execution. When questioned, Jesus as
the incarnate Son admits his kingship to Pilate. It
is the accusation of the Jewish leadership, which
knows that to appropriate this title without Roman
permission is a capital crime. But Jesus confesses
as well that he possesses no worldly power, no le-
gion of followers to stand up in violent defense
of its king. Jesus tells Pilate instead that his mis-
sion is to *testify to truth*. Pilate, the man of power
at this hour, finds this declaration mildly absurd

and dismisses it with his famously cynical question: "What is truth?" (Jn 18:38). The incapacity of the Roman governor to engage the question of truth, his powerlessness to lean forward and know more, contrasts sharply with his domineering awareness of holding the thin thread of another man's life in his hands. "Do you not know that I have power to release you, and power to crucify you?" (Jn 19:10). For Pilate, his own power is the only truth of the hour, the decisive power he wields to spare this life or not. The moment is a genuine epiphany. It manifests the radical dominion over truth that power in this world will exercise in the centuries after Christ. To this day truth remains vulnerable before worldly power, threatened and derided, subject to rebuff and disdain and even violent death, if it gets in the way of worldly power. In triumphant materialism, in technological expertise and obsession, Pilate's dismissal is still heard. And yet, as always, the pure gaze of faith and the contemplative path of prayer quietly offer an indisputable assurance of the inviolability of lasting, eternal truth.

～

At this point in modernity, a deeply ingrained antagonism to an authority of truth beyond self has become a serious obstacle to religious faith.

Determining truth for oneself has replaced a need to receive truth from the unquestioned authority of religious tradition. For many people, questions of ultimate religious import, if they are a concern at all, must be decided without interference, exclusively for themselves. And that often means an idiosyncratic formulation, an amalgam of vague religious notions culled and constructed from disparate sources. It is the truth for oneself that alone matters, if truth is sought at all. Religious conviction in this view is a purely private matter. The primary reason behind this is not an advancement in critical understanding. It is rather the modern resistance to the act of faith. Acceptance of the doctrinal truth of Christianity has always demanded the humility of a submission in faith in order to receive a transcendent truth that must be given to us. Pride and a self-sufficient intelligence make this humble submission unappealing, if not impossible.

∿

It is an opposite orientation by which contemplative life prospers. The contemplative soul thrives only by a reception of truth from a source in the Church, which requires, not just the soul's faith, but an act of love. Submission in faith to the doctrinal truth of Christianity is a loving act, which deepens precisely in prayer. Truth for a contemplative is never a discovery simply from searching and effort: it comes always as a gift. More intensely, perhaps, than an ordinary believer, the contemplative is aware that faith is a great gift and that the reception of truth depends necessarily on a source for truth. The contemplative's love for truth cannot be separated from a love for the Church and for the vast witness to truth embodied in the Church's teaching. The common disposition of a true contemplative to prostrate the soul in awe and gratitude and humble submission before Catholic teaching reflects this attitude of dependency. Truth is embraced only in love and must be received always in humility.

～

Submission in the presence of truth is not an exacting demand. For the yearning for truth burns in the human soul and finds satisfaction whenever truth is finally met. This yearning is a flame that cannot be extinguished. Despite all human effort to deny the existence of God, or simply to live without concern for the question of God, a complete indifference to the truth of God is impossible. Even without admitting so, the human soul hungers to know who God is, just as a child wants to know his own father and mother. At best, man can only avert attention from a question that may seem to have no solution or answer. By its very nature, the contemplative life has the reverse effect: it inflames the soul's thirst for truth. Indeed, there is no contemplative grace bestowed unless a soul plunges deeply into a craving for truth. Over the course of time, the contemplative becomes a soul consumed by a desire for truth. Every falsity and artificial mask, every compromise that leans away from truth, every contrived and convenient inter- pretation that strays from truth, is inimical to con- templative life. This is not at all surprising, nor does it require strenuous effort. The turning each day to what is real and true becomes a natural impulse for the contemplative precisely because God is ul- timate reality and truth. The degree to which our soul lives in truth, in even the simplest of daily tasks and endeavors, conquering pretension and egoism, confronting the truth of our absolute dependency on God, is simply an indirect preparation and readi- ness for all deeper relations with God.

～

A passion for truth cannot be sustained without confronting our incapacity to lay hold of ultimate truths on our own. Truth does not yield its secrets except to those who seek it with humility. And thus the need to recognize a source of truth be- yond self to disclose these deeper secrets. We have to acknowledge that our own search for truth has been preceded by many other seekers of truth. No one searching for ultimate truth can do so in isolation. The truth of Christianity, in particular, cannot be encountered without delving deeply into a tradition of saints and mystics and great theologians. The Church herself in her doctrinal elucidation is essential to the encounter with ultimate truth. Those who resist this demand of deeper assent to their Catholic faith will likely find that their mind, instead of seeking to penetrate the truths of faith, settles into some corner where the satisfactions of an easier knowledge are available. Faith can be washed down and fade in intensity when a more serious engagement with the truths of faith is not part of our prayer. Without serious prayer, the search for the deeper truths of the transcendent order, divinely revealed and metaphysical truths, the truths that never fully unveil themselves to intelligence, loses its appeal after a time. The truths that offer no conclusive gratifications of easy understanding, but continue to provoke and disturb, will no longer seem worth the trouble to seek and ponder.

∽

Without a yearning for truth cultivated and deeply embedded in our character, we can easily be swept up in current intellectual fashions. Novelty and innovation exercise a powerful appeal. The rupture with old ways and old thinking, the replacement of them with the new, is not just an intellectual act. A subtle inclination of rebellion is often taking place. The desire to be independent in one's thinking and in one's decisions has a seductive quality, especially for the young. But often what parades outwardly as independence in thought is simply an unreflective need to embrace the ruling opinions of the time. When no critical faculty is exercised from a source deeper in the soul, it is easy to fall under the sway of views disdainful of older traditions. In the religious realm, this is often disastrous. The incapacity to perceive sacred questions in the truths of religion leads sometimes to a permanent loss of interest in religious faith. At some point a soul must have, on the contrary, a profound experience of the sacred, which by its nature is always an incomplete taste, provoking a desire to know more. This need is fundamental for religious faith. The contemplative life in one sense is an ongoing intensification of this initial encounter with sacredness. The indestructible drawing power of the sacred, rooted in changeless truth, carries the contemplative life forward. Intellectual fashion will seem quite unsubstantial and flimsy against this far deeper attraction for the soul.

∼

A profound need to resolve once and for all the question of God as a personal reality: Why does this need not drive every soul? If it can be ignored so readily, does this suggest that many people are simply uninterested in ultimate religious questions? Or does this indifference reflect a certain spiritual sloth and a preference to evade the hard search for religious truth? Another possibility, a form of wishful thinking, would also seem likely. Perhaps many people think that their own decision alone determines the reality or unreality of God. In this view, there is no God if one commits to a conviction of his non-existence. The existence of God depends solely on believing or not believing in him. Without one's personal belief, he has no basis to exist. If I choose to consider God an impossibility, he simply cannot exist. My personal conviction determines God's existence and settles the matter. Without arguing explicitly in this manner, it would seem that many people adopt this line of thought, despite its illogic. The obvious possibility that the existence of any reality beyond ourselves does not require our conviction in order to be quite real, and the serious consequence this might entail if the reality in question is God, does not seem to occur to them. They have made their wager; it is enough. The contemplative must find in this tragic conclusion a great and painful provocation.

~

Many young people today seem to understand the search for truth to be a kind of creative process. One formulates a philosophy of truth as a personal project that is ongoing and provisional, subject to alteration and modification as life continues. One can add or remove items according to one's shifting taste and need. Nothing is definitive and lasting, nothing is so solid and determined that it cannot be retracted after a time. There is always the possibility to retrace one's steps. The creative dynamic rules and exerts a dominant pressure toward change and flexibility. Just as an artist can cover over his canvas and paint anew, one who forges his own understanding of truth can always rethink commitments and alter them. It is rare, therefore, that moral principles in a personal philosophy of this sort translate into fixed and binding obligations. It is the nature of a purely personal understanding of truth to be negotiable and open to review. If one faces an exceptional need, the necessary justification can be found without great effort or anxiety. A personal philosophy of truth proves convenient in such exigencies. One can always return honor to a principle after a choice that contradicts it has been completed.

~

For all the posturing of intellectual courage in religious skepticism, the claim is superficial in comparison to the fortitude of someone who holds tenaciously to belief while undergoing a trial of faith. The anxious passion of the soul that gropes and stumbles in striving for truth, in clinging to God, when all is silent and in shadow is true courage. Such a soul cannot be said to prefer a comfortable illusion. Rather, a decision to believe, despite the experience of dark obscurity, lived to its unseen end, without turning back, is rooted in a love for truth. That choice, when it is passionate for God, can be both the great drive and the great agony of a life. The claim, on the contrary, of a courageous act by those who cast off religious belief is a pretense and exaggeration. This may be little more than a disguise for avoiding the harder demands that accompany a life of faith. Intellectual indifference to religious questions is for many people a contrived attitude, an imitation of a supposed sophistication that must be adopted among educated people toward religious matters. It is often in reality an indulgence in cowardice and intellectual sloth. Just the opposite is seen in the souls of great faith, who are energetic souls always. The darkness they sometimes experience in faith goads them to live their faith in a more intense witness of generosity. Precisely when the feeling of God seems overcome by shadow and cloud, their activity is often more heroic. Their faith is lived at a deeply personal level; it is not just a commitment of the mind to unquestioned truths.

∼

The idea that we arrive at truth only by some form of method, by following set procedures, by rules of verification that alone confirm the existence of a truth—this may be a common misunderstanding of truth today. In this view, a claim to truth has no value unless it can meet the ruling standards in place for validating a truth. The contemporary notion of truth is confined largely to certainties regarding the physical universe discovered by means of empirical testing. The idea that any truth exists apart from an empirical observation is understood to be a misuse of the word truth and a misconception. What religious people call truth is therefore a confusion of terminology. In this view, "religious" truth is an oxymoron, a misappropriation of the word. A religious truth is at best a preference for a hypothetical conjecture. It is to assert an unverifiable claim regarding an undiscoverable world. Religious conviction as such has no claim to truth for anyone who does not adopt it. Assertions of a religious nature are purely subjective espousals of idiosyncratic value. They may possess some semblance of reality for a particular person, but only within the inner domain of a personal psychology. This internal reality has no necessary connection to what actually exists or does not exist outside the narrow confines of an individual mind. The destructive dismissal of religious truth in this manner reflects not just a professional animus of scientists. The problem today is the more dangerous one of a common cultural education in the understanding of truth that leads exclusively to irreligious conclusions.

∼

The impoverishment of truth to a mere knowledge of facts and information is to truncate the mind from its natural hungers. When truth has no meaning other than to possess correct information and to make accurate observations, the mind suffers an unnatural closure within itself. Perhaps it does not realize the degrading of its own natural capacity. The hunger for truth will then diminish to a search for mere fragments of reality, a sifting among particles and pieces of knowledge instead of a broader exploration seeking the unbounded whole of reality. There is an implicit hopelessness in this refusal to ponder more serious questions of truth. The hopelessness rests on a conviction that no such deeper truth exists. And so the mind limits itself to superficial satisfactions, adding endless acquisitions to its knowledge, but never drawn to the deeper quest for wisdom and ultimate supernatural truth. The worst consequence of these self-imposed restrictions on intelligence is that God is never sought, never encountered. It is easier to consider God a question without an answer and to bury him in a category of irrelevance. The truth of the soul and its existence beyond this life likewise goes unexamined. It is more comfortable to assume that nothing awaits us after death. The dismissal of God has already imposed an inevitable conviction of a final end to our existence at death. Both these denials offer an attractive release. For there is no need then to question too vigorously one's personal conduct in this life. And in that sense the narrow reduction of truth to a tightly restricted notion is a tragically attractive option for many secularized minds. It is a spiritual choice that many make and then retain for a lifetime with a firm commitment.

∼

The restriction of truth to a narrow standard obtained by scientific verification naturally has serious religious implications. Perhaps the most unnoticed consequence is to dismiss the importance of tradition from the notion of truth. Science has little need for tradition as such. Scientific advancement presses forward by fresh discoveries, continually leaving the past behind. There is a steady need to discard and replace what has become obsolete. The current state of knowledge is inevitably superseded by new developments and refinements. Tradition has therefore no great importance in the realm of science and technology; rather, it is often equivalent to what is antiquated and archaic, what is no longer useful or in use. Tradition in science possesses only at best a historical interest. If one refers to a tradition in the distant past linked to contemporary research, it is likely to be a tradition littered with false views and erroneous theories that were subsequently corrected. There are very few past scientific achievements that remain of immediate usefulness in the present. If a tradition of scientific achievement is studied, it is not to perceive any truth in itself, but only to understand the progress over time that led to the current advanced state of a science. This mentality that detaches tradition from any connection to truth is disastrous if applied to religious truth. The truths of faith can be received only from a sacred tradition. The tradition in this case does not become dated and obsolete; it does not give way and collapse in the face of new developments. Yet in subtle ways, many people are affected by the technological mentality that sees in what is ancient nothing that can claim an

unalterable value. The notion of abiding and absolute truth, unchanging and unchangeable, is anti-
thetical to many modern minds.

~

The manner in which we daily engage the sacred
notion of truth is bound to affect our prayer. This
is not simply a question of whether we live in a
proper relationship with reality. Truth is ultimately
the presence of God, but of course we cannot have
contact with God in the way we encounter tangible realities. The truth of God can only be encountered more deeply as we extend our engagement
with truth to a deeper level of receptivity. In that
sense, we can say that an effort to understand the
truth of any particular reality is not equivalent to a
reception by our soul of truth in itself. The greater
reality of truth in itself extends beyond every frag-
mentary, isolated, and partial encounter with any
particular reality we experience. It is an encounter
with the mystery of existence in itself. By contrast,
the search to know any real particular thing is often to some degree analytical, dissecting, investiga-
tive. It is the mode of research, intent on discovery.
The second contact with the truth of existence as
a mystery in itself cannot insist solely on discovery
or make it the exact goal of the mind's yearning.
Contact with the wonder of existence in itself at

this second level requires a contemplative silencing of the mind, keeping it alert and attentive and open to receive. A patience of the mind must be cultivated to engage the deeper mystery of existence. This demands a refusal to stop at only partial knowledge, a refusal to limit our attention to merely useful knowledge, a refusal to satisfy ourselves only with the knowledge of the senses. This second manner of using the mind is ultimately necessary for the sacred encounter with the mystery of God. His existence can shake our soul with the certitude of real presence when we have in effect prepared ourselves for this encounter. This takes place often by confronting the sacredness of real existence in created things with a refined spirit of silent receptivity.

3

Contemplative Intimations

"Because He has first known us, He has left, from His glance, a certain power deep down in us, whereby we can in turn know Him."

—Charles Journet

"We do not always know how to embrace the most pregnant truth, which must slowly produce its fruit in us."

—Henri de Lubac, S.J.

"Once a man's soul has been brushed in passing by this burning wing, it becomes a stranger everywhere. It may fall in love with things, it will never rest in them."

—Jacques Maritain

The rebuttal to every antagonism to religious truth cannot be mainly by way of intellectual argument. If there is an essential rebuttal, it is in the experiential certainty of God that is given in faith. The contemplative life by its nature displays an enhanced intensity of this certitude of God. For contemplatives, it would seem laughable, absurd, preposterous to suggest that God does not exist. The years of mysterious and sacred contact with him are too significant and strong. The yearning for God in their soul has gradually become the irrefutable realization of his presence near their soul. Long before the contemplative becomes deeply aware of this truth, however, there are always intimations of his personal presence. These are gifts that must be recognized if a soul is to be seized by a deeper hunger for prayer. And in many cases, the secret expressed to a life by the hints of divine presence is a quiet one. Nonetheless, it is never completely undetectable, and any soul that crosses a threshold to a passion for prayer can look back at many encounters that reveal the presence of God in other lives and naturally in one's own life.

At some point in every contemplative life, God speaks a secret, which he then continues to repeat. But throughout a lifetime, the secret remains not entirely heard; the whisper of it is always too soft. Nonetheless, from the beginning of contemplative graces, the soul senses the personal invitation and starts to taste a hunger for God that cannot be assuaged. Once that hunger is roused, it provokes a hidden intensity of love within a soul that no other person will be able to perceive except partially. All deeper love, as in marriage, has this quality of secrecy. Such love is utterly personal, directed to a single other, exclusive and particular in its focus. Only the beloved can know the passion of love that another soul possesses for it. When this love is a contemplative passion for God, it penetrates beyond the ordinary boundaries of separation between persons. The union has no limits, and this truth of endless encounter with God is the ongoing taste of the secret spoken by God to the soul. Moreover, God himself cannot but respond with a return of love when a soul is inflamed with desire for divine love, and this, too, is an element of this great secret received from God. These contemplative lives come to know in the privacy of their heart not only that God loves, but that their own love moves him. Their longing for God becomes a way of knowledge, and it takes them increasingly over time in a secret manner into the heart of God.

~

Perhaps without exception God declares some form of a secret to a soul when he desires a special offering from it. In some cases this secret is a dramatic experience, like Blaise Pascal's famous night of recognition when he encountered, not the God of the philosophers, but the living God of Abraham, Isaac, and Jacob. Afterward Pascal sewed a short, written testimony of the event into his outer coat and kept this secret concealed for the rest of his life. He understood that it could not be shared with another person, that the temptation to speak of it must be refused. Released indiscreetly to probing and evaluation, it would surely become tarnished. A doubt might even arise whether anything so personal and private from God was ever expressed. Foreign eyes examining it, interpreting it, glancing at it in curiosity, would risk emptying it. Once the sacredness was lost, there would be no recovery. The written words might remain, but the deeper mystery beneath the words would vanish. We, too, must listen for God speaking a secret to our soul. And then we must take that secret to a hidden place near our heart, keeping it for remembrance, letting it burn as a perpetual flame.

~

What is the nature of such a secret? Is it of the mystical order? A message comparable to a private revelation received by a seer? Nothing so exalted is likely, nor is it necessary. It would seem that God prefers plain speech with most souls, even in communicating a personal secret. An occasion outwardly unstartling, without preparation, is more probable. The quiet of a church in an empty hour is a possibility. Yet even in the ordinary setting, the encounter with God can be indisputable, engraving a permanent memory. One thing seems common to all such secrets. They cut the heart from the first hour and draw blood. They cause a pain that continues at unpredictable intervals because not all has been understood at once; there has been only a partial comprehension. The pain over time of carrying a private secret from God is in what is not fully known, not yet understood, to some extent closed to our awareness. And so there is a hunger for silence in the soul that recognizes that a secret has been given to it. There is a need to pray with this secret enclosed in the silence of the heart, the better to hear it, closer to its whisper and the sacred invitation it contains.

~

A companion who listens for a tone of voice rather than to words alone, who perceives in our eyes a communication not ready for speech, who understands a truth we want to express when it has not arrived at clarity to our confused soul—this is the nature of deeper friendship. Friendship of this nature implies a need to be known by another and, at times, the selfless attention of another. But there is another kind of friendship. The secret gaze of God upon our soul can be an exquisite form of friendship, incomparable to any human relations. God's friendship conveys a mysterious awareness that someone sees a truth in our soul that we do not yet recognize in ourselves. It must occasionally shock us that a secret beauty exists in us that we cannot perceive but is known to God.

～

If we are fortunate, we have experienced the abrupt silence of a very prayerful person and have been puzzled by it. This silence is not natural reserve or shyness or a sign of displeasure at the turn of a conversation. Something different seems to be taking place. Without warning, for no obvious reason, the person turns quiet, even in familiar company. Suddenly no desire seems to breathe in that soul but to remain in silence, no choice except this incapacity for speech. Perhaps a recognition has emptied the appeal of words, and silence is all the soul wants at that moment. Who can say in observing from the outside? In any case, it is clear that the silence hides a secret. We cannot know what it might be; the secret is concealed. We can only remain outside wondering what has taken his attention so captive. He looks like a child who has heard a mother or a father calling from home and then sets off without delay. The soul seems to be answering a clear summons from another, returning to a companionship closed to our eyes.

～

He was a quiet man, but in a deeply spiritual manner. Always near him, like an invisible companion, there was a silence, even when he was immersed in external activity or surrounded by noise. He seemed to protect and savor a deep quiet in his soul, and in that sense he had the soul of a monk. He would not forsake this quiet; it was clearly loved, almost like the love a man has for his child after losing by some tragic circumstance the mother of that child. And so he carried this silence everywhere, as a man might carry this special child, into every conversation and to every place. It was present even when he was not silent, for he often seemed to speak his words from a region of the soul that is not customary in people. For that reason, the significance of his words was often not recognized at once. He was saying more than a first response could capture, and I am not sure even he realized it. In his later years, this form of wisdom had become natural for him. His words were plain and simple, but then at times they assumed almost a foreign nuance, a subtlety of meaning not usual in common conversation. His words on those occasions were heard better after refusing a quick understanding or an easy interpretation. It was only later that a deeper meaning was understood. Once, for instance, he said he never found any of his deeper desires satisfied and yet he was never discontent. The meaning received at such times was more a glimpse of something that was quickly covered over and returned to concealment than any truth clearly exposed and open now to examination.

～

Despite our good intentions and efforts to serve God in works, we risk never going very far in our relations with God if we assume our external activities are the exclusive measure of our identity before God. Who we are before the eyes of God is, rather, a secret, interior truth. This secret truth will remain unknown to us, unsuspected, never discovered, unless we have a serious need for prayer in our lives. Silent prayer is a necessity because only then do we sense the deeper reality of an unseen dimension of ourselves known ultimately to God. This hidden truth of ourselves will correspond always to the depth of our soul's longing for God. How intense and consuming is our soul's passion for God? How hungry is our soul for companionship with Jesus Christ? Even if our lives have no dramatic or notable activities to distinguish them, the interior life of a cleaving attachment to God can be great. This is the secret truth of our souls that we can bring before the gaze of God each day. It is the primary focus of the divine gaze of love.

～

The desire for greatness is an essential drive if our soul is to arrive at closeness to God and a contemplative holiness. But of course this hunger for greatness must be understood properly, for it is a compulsive drive also in all egocentric pursuit. The pursuit of greatness in the spiritual realm is different. It is the quest for a secret, hidden offering of self to God. For that reason, it remains to some extent unseen and unrecognized by others, and this is part of its greatness and its beauty. The secrecy of a complete offering of soul to God is likewise indispensable to contemplative life. This pursuit of a heroic gift of oneself to God, for the sake of God alone, is holiness in whatever form it takes. It is the reason why Saint Thomas Aquinas speaks of magnanimity, the noble aspiration to do something great and beautiful for love of God, as the jewel of the virtues. The secret offerings of the magnanimous soul to give all to God are essential acts sustaining a contemplative life.

$\sim$

It is a startling thing to consider how a particular decision, quite insignificant in the hour it takes place, can secretly hide the truth of a spiritual destiny. Without that decision, a completely different life would have been lived. The choice, trivial and optional at the time it occurs, is part of a soul's destiny. An entire life, in other words, can reside at an unsuspected, secret juncture when a seemingly unimportant impulse is obeyed. Once the decision is made, the hour releases the bolt on a great interlocking network of influences and events that would not take place but for that choice. Perhaps we do not pay sufficient attention to the importance of such junctures and crossroads, in which a single choice affects a whole lifetime and, indeed, can lead to a choice for prayer as the sustaining truth of our lives. Perhaps only in later years of life are we inclined to ponder that our entire life was concealed within that hour. The essential direction of our life took its first step there, and all else followed. And this may not seem worth considering until we realize that an unseen divine companion was present in that hour; not only present but gazing from eternity on all that would subsequently follow. That realization is certainly cause for wonder, and perhaps especially so when we understand that a love for prayer as an absolute value commenced in that hour.

∿

As adults after the Second World War, my father and mother both attended a daily morning Mass at a church in Manhattan before going to work each day. Without their knowing it, they were receiving the Body of the Lord together as they would countless times in the coming decades. By his own account, my father at some point found himself distracted in these morning Masses by the presence in another pew of his future wife. With his inevitable smile at the memory, he would comment that his effort to concentrate in prayer was more difficult by the day. His next impulse was to time his departure from his pew after Mass to open the door at the back of the Church in a gentlemanly gesture for the lady. To his consternation, no notice was forthcoming after a few days of the same pattern, and he decided to initiate a conversation. Such an insignificant gesture, a choice that might have been abandoned just as impulsively; and yet what followed was an entire lifetime of very admirable love between these two. And who would deny that Our Lord himself was secretly present and standing near the door in the vestibule of that Manhattan church? Perhaps he also joined to their souls by means of this initial meeting their love always for prayer and the Mass and for the Church.

～

For any serious pursuit of love, and perhaps for any deeper contemplative life, a spiritual act must occur at some point in the presence of someone deeply loved. At an hour chosen by God, our soul's attention must be entirely absorbed in the unique reality of another person who is loved. The sense of love as an irretrievable gift brushes up against us in that hour. A desire for permanence and irreversibility in love awakens in that hour. We realize intuitively that love is not a repeatable experience but must be renewed continually. Never a return to a prior experience, but only increasing degrees of intensity in love can be pursued. The choice to love is known then to contain everything of worth and value. The soul has found the one thing needful. A secret hunger is given to it, and never just for one person alone; it is, rather, a hunger for the God who has extended a glimpse of this irretrievable gift to the soul and is the source of all love and of all deeper love for prayer.

~

Sometimes the richer silence, and the secret it conceals, comes only after a sustained struggle. For a long time the silence in this other man, quite differently, seemed to hide an inner distress, some dark confusion in his soul beyond his strength to control. He was not unhappy in appearance, and his outward demeanor ordinarily gave nothing away. It was only his silence, sometimes protracted and stubborn, that hinted at a deeper concealed struggle. The battle was surely a spiritual one. My guess

is that the time of unbelief in his life had never entirely healed, and the wound remained. Not that he
suffered instability in his faith; there was no sign
of any wavering in him about God and religion.
Every external indication showed clear and fixed
commitments, even willfully and strictly so; he had
no inconstancy in prayer. Yet there was something
unseen and hidden that seemed to cause trouble
for him, some lingering hard stone in his soul that
he could not lay his hands upon to knead and pull
apart for examination and so exorcize. But who
can pull apart a stone? He was a strong-willed man
and for a long time may have thought to conquer
his pain by breaking it down and crushing it. And
then his silence seemed to change, which is to say
that he became quiet in a different way. He seemed
no longer trapped within himself, buried in a deaf
wordlessness. He could be quiet as before, but it
was different now, not painful to observe, not like
someone made mute by an injury. Perhaps he perceived after many years what faith really signifies
after trusting too little in the wonder of this gift.
He may have finally realized the spectral character
of his returning to unbelief again, which I think
may have periodically frightened him. He did not
seem to be carrying any more a sense of private
menace. And so his silence became different; it was
not like sand swept about in a heavy night wind; it
was, rather, like a brisk flow of water lit at dawn,
running down mountain rocks. From that time,

getting old now, he seemed often to seek the quiet of a chapel and sometimes spent hours of his day in front of a tabernacle.

∼

The discovery of a deeper contemplative invitation within ourselves, secret and unknown until that time, may depend at some point on offering ourselves courageously to the Cross of Jesus Christ. The Cross in this sense is not just to accept a suffering we have to bear from external events. We already have had that experience in life. Something different must be understood, a demand for an offering of love, a more complete surrender of ourselves to God than we have previously made. We perhaps can sense that a truth within ourselves will remain untapped and inaccessible without this offering. An unknown part of ourselves awaits an interior act that will release its truth into actual life. But this truth of our deeper being must be surrendered to God in prayer before it comes to life. We cannot really understand what this means until we do it. Precisely by that offering and that greater surrender to God, we discover the deeper secret in our identity that calls us to deeper prayer. This hidden depth has existed in the soul all along without our being aware of it, and finally we see it beginning to come to life.

4

The Contemplative and the Poor

"God touches hearts when we least expect it. . . .
It implies that whoever thinks about it, whoever
has a habit of thinking about it, who is covered by
the stratum of habit, is also the one who is less
exposed and, so to speak, offers less possibility for
the divine approach."

—Charles Péguy

"Sometimes we think we are looking for God. But
it is always God who is looking for us, and he often allows himself to be found by those who are
not looking for him."

—Henri de Lubac, S.J.

"Let us concern ourselves with those who lack everything, those of whom no one thinks. Let us be
the friends of those who have no friends."

—Charles de Foucauld

*For some people the encounter with the poor serves as a
prelude to the contemplative life. This need not be so, but
often it seems the case. We are likely to find that genuine*

contemplatives, even those now in cloisters or monaster-ies, have sought real contact with the poorest of the poor at some stage in their spiritual life. The reason is not so sur-prising. The mysterious presence of the Lord in the poor man draws the beginnings of a hunger in a soul that is not realized at first but soon becomes evident. It is an initial encounter, as the Eucharist itself is, with the sacred mys-tery of God's personal presence. For those who ponder this secret attraction for the poor which begins to take hold in their soul, the consequence is often a desire to plunge more deeply into the search for direct contact with God in prayer. The result is the beginning of a contemplative hunger for prayer that never abandons a soul.

There will always be souls who meet the poor at some point in their lives and find in the encounter, whether they realize it or not, an invitation to a per-manent search for God. They are unable to leave the poor alone once the real misery of a poor per-son has pierced their soul. Even if they are not Christian and have no awareness of Christ's pres-ence in the poor, a desire begins to burn in them to seek out the poor, and this is certainly a grace. This need to be with the poor returns with reg-ularity; it disturbs and draws them, and it leads them to more intense involvement with poor peo-ple. Mother Teresa's houses throughout the world, with the many volunteers they attract, are a testi-mony to this phenomenon. But if this is true even for non-Christian people, what does it reveal of the Gospel promise regarding our own love for the poor? Holiness may never, in fact, permit exception to the demand for some form of personal contact with the poor. The encounter with poor people introduces into our soul the mysterious truth of poverty's stark appeal for all spiritual seeking. It is an initiation into a secret taste and a subsequent longing that cannot be satisfied ever in this life— except by seeking God more intensely. The great truth here is that Jesus himself is hiding in this attraction. And this is the case even for the person who does not yet know Jesus Christ.

~

At some point in life God may invite us, for a period of time, to become a servant to another person, fully at the disposal of the other's great need, subject to stressful and physical demands. It is a summons to forget our own dignity and embrace an inferior position for the sake of love. It may mean answering to arbitrary whims and thankless commands. It can entail physically exhausting ourselves in sacrificial availability to another. At times, in divine providence, this involves care for a family member who has become sick and helpless. Or it may be a patient and steady companionship with someone seriously troubled or suffering a mental breakdown. It may be only after we have accepted for a time the servant's role, relinquishing any option of refusal, that we begin to understand the truth of losing self for God. It can be a very hard challenge in love. But it can also be a threshold into deeper love for God and for prayer. Indeed, how many heroic souls there are who are much closer to God than they realize because they have given themselves as a servant to a loved one in a time of crushing need. What is more noteworthy, however, is how often this experience leads a soul to greater prayer.

∿

Perhaps there has never been holiness or deeper love for prayer unless a soul at some point in life learns to be a servant to the poor. The reason is not just the need to love poor people in loyalty to the Gospel. It is the dramatic reversal that is important in this act, the exchange of places with the poor person, so that the condition of the poor person is now embraced as our own. In this act of becoming a servant to someone who earlier might have received from our generosity to some lesser degree, a contradiction is made, a true reversal. No longer are we in a position of superiority extending a gift to a person in lower circumstances. The reversal is to allow the poor person's need to command a response from our soul as a servant must respond

to a master. It is not, however, an ordinary servant's response that is invoked. The exchange of
places means that we must exercise love in service.
A crucial awareness is given if this act is done in
recognition that the poor man has now become
superior to us—namely, the incompatibility of a
higher love for God without becoming a servant
to the abject and lowly. And why? Because the One
adored and loved became himself the dishonored
one, the forsaken, the poor man. We cannot remain long in that knowledge without experiencing a demand for becoming a servant to the forgotten poor. In many cases, this surges into a desire
that lasts for a lifetime. And in many cases it is the
first impulse of a soul toward the contemplative
pursuit of God. The preference to keep the poor
man's request superior to our own need persists as
a path into the concealed mystery of God.

～

How difficult to let ourselves be captive to a grace
when it is subtle, delicate, more *suaviter* than *fortiter*,
awaiting a recognition at a deeper layer of our soul
beneath emotion. An inward attention to the Lord
is decisive in such recognitions. But this means that
we have some quiet and calm in our interior heart.
God may value such recognitions much more than
we think. Our own inclination is to treat them as

small, inconsequential moments. Yet undramatic, less startling graces may shape and determine the spiritual life in a significant way. The acts that flow from them are not unimportant simply because the grace that provokes them is hardly noticed. Inattentiveness toward *any* grace is in effect to ignore God himself. Many times these graces concern small acts of kindness to forgotten souls, the poor people who ordinarily receive nothing from others. Once we listen to God with a deeper loving silence, we may find that these souls strongly attract us, draw us, provoke our heart. The more we realize God's presence near them, the more we anticipate encounters with them. The opportunity for love seems always to expand as we uncover its hiding place, and we find this hiding place precisely in such souls. In this sense we have to refine our understanding of love. It may be thought that the most difficult actions, those requiring the greatest exertion of energy, are the most decisive in the spiritual life. But it may be otherwise.

∼

Perhaps some people desire a God who would speak only from towering heights and in a voice of ancient thunder that carves fixed pronouncements into granite—and not a God who would speak in quiet whispers to their soul. It may be they do not really want a God who would seek a friendship with them. The thought of a real friendship with God may seem troublesome, intimidating, suitable only for holy persons. And then, at some point in their life, if they have kept their faith and have continued to pray, God may surprise them by entering into their ordinary hours with a shocking immediacy. He will hide, for instance, in the inconvenience of encounters with simple, neglected people that begin to be noticed with unusual regularity. After a while, the person feels as though a voice is repeating "I am here" in a man or woman lying on a city sidewalk. The soul hearing this is never ready for this possibility of God speaking in some shabby corner of pavement where a lonely person resides. Yet the desire of God for recognition apparently does lead him to choose such settings for the whispers of his voice. And a soul must not deny it but must, rather, accustom itself to this manner of speaking from God. No longer will God permit simply a detached look at written words frozen in stone. The soul will have to pay attention to the whispers heard within it and begin to pray differently.

∼

It may be that with every soul God starts with a small request, almost as if asking a favor. It may be small as a request, but the response is in no way negligible in significance. The decision to grant what he wants may affect everything that follows in a life. Think, for instance, of Peter, asked to put out his boat to deeper water and let his nets down for a catch, which he could have refused. Certainly, if acceded to, the small request will be succeeded by more requests. Someone who knows what is at stake might suggest it is a trick on God's part. The initial request is not so hard, never so overwhelming or burdensome. It is a small appeal, just to get a soul started. Nonetheless, people do refuse even this meager request. Not because they are ungenerous; rather, they cannot conceive of God making a minor appeal of this sort. Often in our lives, perhaps, this involves a gesture of charity to a poor person beyond simply a quick, mindless donation. The possibility is worth a moment's attention, for God may certainly be hiding in that small hour. Unfortunately, the idea of God making a request in the person of a beggar is an unpalatable notion for many people. Perhaps a person is not thinking of God at all in such a moment. Nonetheless, Our Lord makes the offer, and it can be ignored. By contrast, the offer can be accepted, and then it includes an invitation, which can be welcomed even without realizing it at the time. Once we respond to a small request from God, especially one that comes from a poor man, an invitation to discover God waiting for us in our soul's silence is bound to arrive in an hour of prayer. Soon enough, if we have given with love to the small request of a beggar, another deeper invitation will be heard in our heart while praying before a tabernacle.

∼

The reluctance to being a servant may explain why many people who have a genuine sympathy for the poor keep their physical distance from them. Getting physically close to a destitute person makes a claim on us, which at the time we ordinarily do not realize. If a person is helpless in his poverty and we draw close enough, we cannot backtrack and walk away without suffering our own callousness. And if we do take some action, it is never an isolated assistance that is soon finished and done with. By a mysterious law that must be written in heaven, if we really do become a servant in love to a particular poor person, he will return to our lives and make fresh demands in unaccountable ways. He will begin to emerge as if from hiding places and assume a presence in our lives that he had not had before. It is a presence that never leaves us for very long. A solicitation of our soul has been initiated, and it begins to disturb our heart with its strange mystery. If we begin to take notice of this truth, we ought also to observe in ourselves a growing desire to be alone with God more often in a place of silent prayer.

~

A narrow and impure vision accompanies all habits of spiritual inattention. When we are distracted and unfocused in our mind, we are easily blind to the realities immediately before our eyes. The consequence is often to neglect a divine request hiding in our encounters with people. Without attentiveness to real souls present before us, speaking to us and returning our gaze, our eyes by a natural weakness tend to indulge in the superficial hungers of mere curiosity. Losing interest in what is before our eyes in fact happens quite easily. Soon we find ourselves impulsively searching for something new upon which to cast our restless eyes. Our days can become an ensemble of hasty, fitful glances rather than a discipline of purposeful and watchful attention. The result is that receptivity to the spiritual reality of other persons diminishes. We perceive little of the actual suffering in a lonely person's face or the features of a person of strong spiritual character. By contrast, these same faces can quickly draw our respect and feeling if we take keener notice. In that case, however, patience must be exercised as well as vulnerability, for we must let ourselves be wounded also in our observations. Granted it can impolite, surely, to gaze too long at another in some circumstances, to linger indiscreetly with our eyes fastened on another, rude and impertinent to peer underneath the sometimes hard features of a troubled human face. Yet cultivating an openness to being moved and wounded when we look at other faces is precisely the humanity to which we must courageously aspire if we are to see as God made our eyes to see. This quality of vision will in turn affect our longing in prayer for the God we cannot see.

～

There can be sometimes a tendency to a certain ethereal quality in souls who otherwise possess refined spiritual interests. Their religious passion is concentrated much on ideas, speculations, spiritual musings. They pursue a religious version of a platonic realm where ideas can be treated as more significant and weighty than actual realities. Religious abstractions draw them as an essential beauty, but these remain abstract attractions, not reaching so far outside the inner solitude of thought. Surely beauty in the mind can be a wonderful thing, but beauty in the mind is not the same as a painting on canvas. Charitable love admired in thought cannot be compared to bending down to a poor and dirty man in the street. Noble aspirations and fine words have value, but they are not equivalent to sacrificial deeds. Every religious person must take care in this regard. Spiritual reflection in quiet hours is a necessary sustenance, but it must lead outward

to hard, concrete demands on our life, or else it
may be an escape from reality. The religious ideal
is chimerical and even deceptive without the steady
labor of sacrificial generosity to others, and especially to the poor. It is love for the poor, in all
disguises of their misery, that draws us to a deeper
love for prayer.

∼

A truly personal encounter with a destitute person
sometimes brings a taste that is bitter before it is
loved. One reason is that the effort to help a poor
person is often an experience of failure, due to our
own ambivalence. We are confused initially by the
combination of physical aversion and the fear we
feel with a need to draw closer. The desire is strong
to extend our hand toward someone who also stirs
our revulsion. Something shouts in our soul to do
something in love, but we are reluctant to dirty our
hands in the effort to love. The touch of our hand
to the dirt of poverty is not easily accepted. And
perhaps it will never be, until we learn the satisfaction it brings of seeing a poor man with different
eyes. For it is not only the poor man in front of
us who is touched. It is then we realize there is no
real love for the poor, and no encounter with the
deeper mystery of contact with the poor, unless we
dirty our hands in the effort to love. Perhaps we
require this experience precisely as a preparation

to face later the more difficult aspects of a deeper life of prayer.

⁓

A form of unrequited love due to our own disregard for the poor may happen more often than we think. It can occur when we show an initial sympathy for a poor person, only to be followed by our own reluctance to go farther in love. Souls who are truly alone, souls cast aside and marginalized, thrown away, are often vulnerable to an additional suffering when some attentiveness is directed their way. The heart that has long been without human love may ignite quickly with a hunger for love when it meets an eye that for a time shows some personal concern. But it may be that we extend an interest to a poor soul only temporarily, soon tiring of the unpleasant, wearying effect that may be carried away from repeated encounters with a particular poor person. Soon enough the same poor soul is avoided, a stranger to our thought and remembrance. And then, too easily, a poor person returns to his former state as an unknown, forsaken entity. Every soul has hungers that never die. It is a sad thing to draw out a poor person's love only to lead the poor person deeper into a conviction of being unlovable. We can remember this, perhaps, if we begin to pray with some commitment and then begin to curtail our practice. Our abandonment of prayer must cause a similar wound to the heart of Jesus Christ.

~

Many people cannot fathom God having gentle eyes for souls who have thrown away their lives in the ruin of a homeless, dissolute life in the city streets. What they do not realize is that the poverty in these souls is sometimes not so different from a quality that draws God to certain saints. In some cases the dissipate wanderings of street people is joined to a conviction within these souls of their worthlessness and irrecoverable loss. They live with a permanent sorrow and regret they are unable to shake. Their own failures are often the cause of this near spiritual despair, and of course there is nothing saintly in this condition. And yet this unrelieved dereliction of soul may draw the divine gaze. Perhaps God sees something close to the same conviction of uselessness in some of his humblest saints. Saint Bernadette, for instance, protested to the presiding bishop at her profession of religious vows to being only good for nothing in the convent. Other saints, like Charles de Foucauld or Francis of Assisi, had a kind of vagabond quality, never finding a lasting home, rootless in the external circumstances of their lives. It is not that God makes no distinctions. The saint is a vastly different soul from a homeless man on the streets. But who knows, God may be attracted by some saints who come very close to a disdain for life's vanities that marks the homeless man in a different way. Perhaps God is attracted as well to the homeless man's absence of worldly self-importance. The consequence may be a great mercy to souls who have no thought of their appeal to God. That thought may help our own prayer when we are carried by God into a greater poverty in our lives.

~

On the last night of his life, never waking, he seemed at first more concealed to me than ever; and yet, strangely, as the night wore on, a contact with him became possible that I had never experienced previously. During the long hours I had alone with him, all the outward vestige of the man became as nothing. In its place another presence began to emerge, stepping out as if from behind shadows and exerting a great attraction. His face drew me into a concentrated gazing. I realized I had never looked carefully at his face before. A sense of spiritual presence hiding within him now consumed my attention, and it made me pray for him. Almost a different identity seemed present, which showed itself in glimpses and then always vanished once more. As I waited for each new appearance in his dying face, he created an intense longing in me. I do not know what I was desiring, only that it was an uncanny strength he exercised over me. I was sure at times he could not depart just now, that his eyes would open before the light of dawn and we would have a conversation. But the waiting in that silence was only a delay. For all I know it was a deliberate delay on his part and for the sake of this silent exchange. At the end he left my soul very lonely for God.

5

Contemplative Kinship with Poverty

"Since the immense blessings of God can only enter and fit in an empty and solitary heart, the Lord wants you to be alone. For He truly loves you with the desire of being Himself all your company."

—Saint John of the Cross

"Only the person who renounces self-importance, who no longer struggles to defend or assert himself, can be large enough for God's boundless action."
—Saint Edith Stein

"Jesus has so taken the last place that no one has ever been able to wrest it from him."

—Abbé Henri Huvelin

Contemplative life cannot escape a relationship with poverty. By the very nature of a deeper hunger for God, poverty is bound to become a spiritual companion to the soul. This does not necessarily mean a life lived in circumstances of grave hardship and deprivation, but it does entail a disappearance from a focus on self. This poverty of a loss of self does not diminish the soul; it arouses a push forward on the path to God. In poverty the contemplative soul discovers that God is truly all that is desired. It inclines these souls as well to a hidden quality in their self-emptying. But the typical tendency to concealment within contemplative lives also makes them indifferent to poverty. They become unconcerned about the cost of poverty, perhaps because their turn away from self makes them inattentive to their experience of poverty. The poverty they experience in placing their life nakedly before God becomes simply unimportant. The essential thing to them is solely their seeking for God.

It takes courage in prayer to choose for oneself the precariousness of poverty. For this choice cannot be made without the risk that some great loss or misfortune might be the eventual outcome. It is a choice in prayer that entails uncertainty and unknown possibilities, and not simply a decision to practice a sacrifice or mortification we can control and determine. It does not mean, for instance, putting on ragged clothes or residing in decrepit surroundings, which may only resemble the external life of a poor man. A poor man's weariness may never be ours to bear. But something else in poverty more uncertain and hazardous might occur. Perhaps we do not realize sufficiently what we may share one day with the poor man—the disregard and scorn he endures, the stripping down of his human dignity, his aloneness in later years. A deeper knowledge of Jesus Christ as the poor man may demand a taste of this poverty. We know his choice to be poor as it begins to belong to our own life. The events, the circumstances of such poverty are unpredictable, impossible to anticipate. There can be no real preparation, only an acceptance that an unsuspected dereliction may at some point enter our lives. Yet there is a promise, too, that a love for the poor Christ will pass a barrier in our heart and attract us as it has many souls in history, like an ancient Christian song reaching across centuries.

~

One wonders what Saint Benedict Labre pondered, the holy beggar of eighteenth-century Rome, when reading his worn Bible in a favorite church up the block from the Colosseum, where he slept on the ground at night, and seeing again the prophetic description of Jesus in Isaiah 53: "He was despised and rejected by men; a man of sorrows, and acquainted with grief; and as one from whom men hide their faces he was despised, and we esteemed him not." These words identify a truth present not just in a holy beggar but in every contemplative life and, indeed, in the Church herself. They must be fulfilled if Jesus is to find a deeper place within our soul for himself and in the Church. How this comes to be, we can leave to God. But it does require accepting that a life of contemplative union with Jesus Christ crucified, when stripped of illusion, must not refuse his humiliations.

~

Serious religious people seem to divide between those requiring encounters with beauty if they are to find strength for long perseverance and those, in contrast, who are drawn to poverty and the starker setting as the more favorable ambiance for meeting God. At first glance, it would seem that these two tendencies could not be combined, as different and even contradictory as they are. And yet the higher spiritual path is to discover their compatibility. The question remains, however, whether one tendency can claim a priority over the other. Which must be sought first? It may in fact be essential for a true contemplative life that an esteem for poverty in our pursuit of God precede the appreciation for beauty. When the enjoyment of beauty becomes linked to religious fervor, it perhaps rarely leads to a love for poverty. But when poverty is loved and a soul learns to be satisfied with less, beauty will soon accompany this love. The beauty that poverty learns to savor, however, is not primarily an aesthetic appreciation. Instead, the beauty of the desert draws the soul made poor, the beauty of the open sky at night, of the slant of sunlight in a shadowed room, of the austere chapel and its tabernacle—all this is found to be enough. It is a real beauty that is discovered in the spare, unadorned settings of poverty, a beauty, it would seem, more conducive to a soul's encounter with the hidden presence of God.

~

No soul is inclined to the "hidden life" of contemplation unless it has begun to love interior poverty with some intensity. A hidden life attracts only at the same time that interior poverty draws the soul with a mysterious appeal. Indeed, the desire to disappear before God's eyes in hiddenness is itself an expression of a growing love for spiritual poverty. This simultaneous desire for hiddenness and poverty is essential to a contemplative life. They together set the contours of territory within the inner spirit for meeting God. They together make the soul a fitting and hospitable place for an encounter with God. Something akin to an inward homelessness then invades the soul, requiring a constant wandering in search of God. And it is in that poverty of interior homelessness that God extends contemplative favors. His preference is not to seek us in a secure location where our soul can return easily for comfort and recovery. He wants us to journey to a place of interior poverty that is hidden from our own recognition and must be sought constantly. The hidden poverty within the soul is where the contemplative soul finds a permanent home—much as nomadic tribes seek their ever-changing home in the expanses of the desert. The place of contemplative encounter with God is a vast interior desert—poor and hidden from outside eyes, concealed for a greater immolation.

~

In their unsettled, shifting experiences of relations with God, contemplative lives are marked by intense paradoxes. These lives burn and smolder, flame up and descend back again to ashes. Sometimes, surely, God is near and painfully close, but his proximity is never a lasting peace. God seems to be watching from a hiding place, yet every glance toward a location comes up empty, and the soul discovers nothing. The divine face is never identified; rather, what is more certain is the shadowed remembrance of repeated disappearances. On some days, the voice of God in silence seems unmistakable and direct, and then there is the deafening interlude of extended, unbearable silence. The Lord is quick sometimes in answering a small request and then shows indifference to the more passionate plea. These experiences contradict every easy notion of closeness with God. And yet they are the reality of a contemplative soul's intimacy with God in poverty. When a soul is faithful in its surrender to God while undergoing this mingling of disparate experiences, it advances in contemplative love. It may seem that God is shredding and slicing the soul into pieces, but this is not so. He is gradually drawing it to a conclusive and final surrender in poverty that will bring an end to this shifting pattern.

～

At first glance it seems inexplicable that souls favored by God with contemplative graces are often of no account in the world, unfit for any importance, easily ignored, useless and ineffective for more noteworthy achievements. This is not always true, but sometimes it certainly is. There is an irony here that has marked all of Christian history. Perhaps we may think that the perennial existence in Christianity of solitary vocations in monasteries is because this is a proper setting for a life dedicated entirely to prayer. But this may not be the real providential reason for the phenomenon throughout centuries of solitary lives in the deserts and monasteries. The primary reason may rather be that solitude reduces drastically the opportunities for indulging in any self-importance. And this is precisely a necessity for contemplative life, that the soul has no compelling need to leave any trace of its own importance upon the world. But this means also that contemplatives surely hide sometimes in the world, outside the walls of monasteries. These souls find their way somehow to hidden corners where there will be no great accomplishment for the world to admire. Their destiny is to offer themselves fully to God, and everything else in their lives is secondary to that. Their insignificance is in the eyes of the world, but not in God's. They are a sign of the unseen holiness God values perhaps more than visible works that too often glory in their own achievement.

⁓

Almost it would seem an instinct of nature, the manner in which contemplatives flee from attention to themselves. But perhaps it is not so much a flight or an escape as a profound inclination they are following. What we see externally as their tendency to self-effacement and concealment reflects a desire to be released from concern for self. This desire to be free of self burns within their interior prayer. The turn from attention to themselves becomes in their prayer an effort to absorb themselves in someone else. This consuming need to seek an unseen beloved is the truth they are ever desiring in prayer. The tendency to effacement that we may observe in them is not, then, primarily a rejection of interest directed to their own person. Their prayer has had this subtle and lasting repercussion on their personality. They are not content in prayer unless they have disappeared from their own eyes. For they have known that it is only at those times when they are more deeply hidden from their own eyes that their beloved takes their soul captive. And this they are always seeking with yearning and a consuming desire. The turn away from self simply carries over into their life outside of silent prayer.

~

If we desire contemplative graces, maybe we should look at times to place ourselves in unfamiliar settings that deprive us of the easy confidence we acquire when too long in the comfort and security of one place. This willingness to accept risks can refer as much to an effort in external activities, such as a more direct involvement with the poor, as in any change in a location of living. More intense love may only thrive in the face of challenges for which there is no prior experience and no preparation and where the risk of failure or humiliation is a real prospect. At such times we cannot rehearse how we are going to act. We have no clear guidelines. But we may learn something spiritually

important in this uncertainty. Many times in our
lives God may want us to break free of conven-
tional routines and take risks, even if that means
initially stumbling and tripping while performing
in a manner not always to our liking. Advancing
in contemplative love is not a venture in success-
ful achievements. It may not always bring immediately happy experiences. But love, even the effort
of love, always leads us somehow to God, and what
else matters?

~

It is good to seek contemplative life, but not as
though this meant achieving a spiritual status or el-
evation or even a basic proficiency in prayer. The
idea that contemplation could be at one's personal
disposal and available on demand is an obvious misconception. The only proper expectation is that the
soul's yearning to love God has come from God and
cannot be fruitless. A soul becomes contemplative
on the condition that it takes seriously a need in
love to give itself in a complete surrender to God.
Those who persevere in this self-offering will find,
however, that there can be no sense of success or
achievement in seeking to give our soul to God.
The contemplative life requires, rather, the abandonment of all pretense of personal accomplishment. It likely means an experience of the con-

trary, becoming a more emptied person, perhaps a forsaken and useless person. The true contemplative in the last resort has no basis for a recommendation, no résumé, and relies only on a beggar's appeal for credentials.

~

Do religious people of high self-confidence somehow imply by their external bearing a spiritual contradiction? Is it possible that one who loves God, and searches intently for him, can be only full of assurance in all choices? Or is it nearer to the truth that when a soul is closer to God and indeed becoming contemplative, there is more likely to be at times a tentativeness, a restlessness, a questioning directed at self, precisely because in the privacy of the soul in its relations with God a loss is continually taking place? This is a loss and stripping of self that can leave our soul groping at times for an answer, unsettled, uncertain of itself, in large part because we are unsure exactly what God is asking of us. Not always, it seems, does the advancement of a soul in relations with God bring immediate courage and clarity and shining luster. The spiritual life is a journey of varied experiences that include fits and starts and stumbling steps as well as times running with the rush of the wind at one's back.

And yet a life truly seeking God is mysteriously of one piece. Nonetheless, the harmonious interplay of the contrasting experiences over a lifetime may be recognized only at the end. What we will recognize perhaps is that every impoverishment of our lives opened a path to a deeper surrender to God.

∽

There is indeed an "exigency of poverty" demanded by contemplative life: the need to push beyond the familiar and the recognizable, to cross thresholds into unknown realms of rootlessness and insecurity, to stretch the desires of the soul toward longings that cannot be satisfied. Contemplative love can never seek to rest in a semblance of stability. The idea that it can be assured of its next encounter with God is a contradiction to its true longings. It does not seek to arrive at satisfaction in its relations with God or a predictable way of finding him. Rather, it accepts as perfectly natural being cast back upon its own incapacity to encounter God. It has found in a condition of homeless interior poverty the usual location for any meeting with God. But this sense of rootlessness unleashes as well an urgency to give to God always more of itself, even with nothing at hand to give. The gift must be without planning or preparation, always going beyond what has been offered to that point in life.

~

Only in poverty does the inner life of our soul become more completely accessible to God. Before that we are rich to some extent and thwarted from realizing our actual need for God. We will always have obstacles blocking entry to God as long as we have not yet become poor. Even if the truth of our inner poverty has been tasted, it remains a fragile recognition. For our soul to continue in a condition of accessibility to God, nothing possessive in our desire is permitted; no holding on, no effort to retain and keep back can take place. We must trample down all desire to secure protection from our own state of need before God. To be spiritually poor is to be open and unguarded, exposed to new and greater destitution. It is perhaps only at times of real poverty that God carves greater depth into our soul. And he does this primarily by intensifying a desire for himself that we cannot satisfy ourselves. We realize then more deeply the true meaning of having nothing in ourselves but what he extends to us in love.

~

We must learn in prayer a blind confidence in love that impoverishes our soul. Without this confidence, the poverty of contemplative love is likely to stifle our soul's impulse to self-offering. Many times it can seem that we receive nothing in return for the offering of ourselves to God, but we must ignore this. The confidence is a form of hope, an upsurge of strength linked to our faith. It must be exercised with a kind of diligent commitment. Then we are able to choose to continue offering ourselves to God, not for a satisfaction of love, but rather for the self-emptying that accompanies love. We learn to trust an aspect of the encounter with God contrary to every contradiction in our experience of what love should be. For contemplative love brings much more experience of poverty than that of satisfaction. The exercise of confident hope in the eventual fruitfulness of this poverty is a necessity for intensifying our desire for loving God.

～

The contemplative soul comes to accept the impermanent and incomplete nature of all its striving. This realization leads it, not to a spirit of resignation or to an abandonment of its search, but rather to a more humble and poorer seeking. It knows it will find no stable satisfaction or rest in this life. A sense of insufficient striving for love will always goad it, as it no doubt has done to the present day. But a contemplative soul lives in hope of eventual arrival despite experiencing the poverty of its efforts. It knows that a genuine encounter with God is often realized only after it has occurred. The conviction of such concealed meetings drives the contemplative onward, led by deeper inextinguishable yearnings in the soul.

6

Affinity for the Full Gift of Self

"Return to God what He has given you and gives you each day. It seems you want to measure God by the measure of your own capacity, but it will not be so. Prepare yourself, for God desires to grant you a great favor."

—Saint John of the Cross

"Does God give me such wishes so that I may sacrifice them to him or so that I may carry them out?"

—Charles de Foucauld

"The steepest roads are often the best and quickest. The traveler is less inclined to loiter on the way up."

—René Voillaume

No one becomes contemplative except in placing a great value on the gift of their entire self to God. This urge to extend oneself in a generosity of self to God is present no doubt in all holiness. But in the contemplative life it is an essential tendency. Nonetheless, it is helpful to reflect on

what it means to offer a complete gift of ourselves before
God. While the contemplative comes to understand a self-
giving to God as a necessity for the soul, the realization
is also present that nothing truly possessed by self is ever
actually given. All that is given to God is a return of what
already belongs to him. The need to give is also the need to
receive from God what we can only return in love to him.
Only what has been given by God to us can be returned
as a genuine gift to him. This is indeed the very nature of
a deeper surrender in love to him.

The incongruence and folly of extending a donation to God is perhaps not often acknowledged.
With God we cannot make donations. A donation
implies both a benefactor and a partial gift. It usually involves a form of calculation based on what
we can afford to contribute while still holding back
a portion for ourselves. In human settings, a donation can naturally represent a legitimate gift to
someone in need. But a donation even then is a gift
that entails giving just a part of what we possess,
and often not much at all, and sometimes giving
more for our own satisfaction, which amounts to a
teasing and flirtation with real love. God has no desire or need for donations. This is why the Gospel
points always to the complete gift and implicitly
warns against satisfying ourselves with donations.
It is striking that the places in the Gospel where
Jesus is clearly moved with admiration for a soul

have to do with some form of a fully surrendered gift. When the centurion who returns home believing in Jesus' word of healing for his servant, this is an act of absolute, unquestioning trust. He gives himself in this act in a complete manner. When the poor widow tosses her only remaining coins into the temple treasury, this is an act of complete, generous offering. When Mary of Bethany pours out all her perfume, this is a gesture of complete giving. All of these people are praised by Jesus. On the other hand, the partial gift, the incomplete gift, draws an implicit reproach because it stops short at a donation and may resent even this. It is possible, surely, to imagine the rich young man, saddened by Jesus' challenge to give up *all* his possessions, reaching into his money purse and flinging a fistful of Roman coins in the direction of the Lord's feet as he turns to walk away.

∽

Nothing strictly of our own possession can be made a genuine gift to God. Only what we recognize as already belonging to him can be given back to God as a true gift. When we make a gift of anything to God, it is only the return of what has never really belonged to us and was never ours to keep. We give back to God what we finally realize is already his possession. This may seem to contradict the notion of giving a gift. For a gift usually implies a personal possession that is freely handed over to another. But in giving anything to God, the ownership was never ours. A gift offered to God may sound in this way more like the return of a long overdue loan than the generosity generally associated with making a gift. But in truth, we do make a gift, as long as we realize that it is a gift of what has been given to us. We return, not what has been loaned and then is owed, but what is freely ours to give. For we can also refuse a gift to God, which does not signify that anything that could have been given to God now reverts back to our permanent possession. It simply means that we cling to something and withhold it, to our own detriment. All this ultimately does not have to do with the possessions we may accumulate in our lives. It has to do with the surrender of ourselves that we can offer to God. The gift we make to God in surrendering ourselves to God is a gift that completes his gift to us. And what we are surrendering is mysteriously then returned to us, which is the nature of love itself.

∼

The request of a beggar in need is the essential condition for all entry into deeper prayer. We may not at first value this parallel. Perhaps our own attitude is to look upon contact with a beggar as an inconvenient encounter. Even in giving, we may do so reluctantly, in a hurried manner, proceeding quickly on our way. On the other hand, this may not be true in an hour of compassion, when our heart is moved with pity. Then the beggar is seen in all his vulnerability, a tired and lonely figure, heavy in his despair. There is a parallel to this image when it comes to prayer. It may be that thresholds are crossed in prayer because God sees a weary beggar in us and cannot resist our plea in that hour. But we must be willing to beg and plead, and this is not a pleasant act. It seems that only a long perseverance in asking for the grace of deeper prayer turns our request at last into a gift that God cannot refuse.

~

When the Bridegroom comes after a long delay apart from us, he often takes from us something that is hard to give away, something not expected. Every preparation to give ourselves completely to him until this moment can appear very feeble and ineffective before this next request from him. The pattern seems to repeat itself continually in the contemplative life. No learning, no accumulated experience, can counter the shock of losses that cannot be anticipated but that quickly happen in our return to a day's tasks after prayer. There is no exercise or method of protection to offset this pain when his

return is accompanied by a request for a sacrifice
we had not realized was about to be asked of us.
Yet in the end, every loss belongs to God's choice
to draw us into greater love. Sooner or later this
truth has to be embraced with a singular conviction if we are to advance in the life of contemplative prayer.

~

"A gratuitous act is one that is *given for nothing*"
(Raïssa Maritain). The contemplative life demands
this tending toward gratuity, this looking to give
with no expectation of return, empty of any desire
for self. We receive from God only to the degree
that we give ourselves away. Yet what is received
from God is not a return at all of what has been
given away. What we receive instead is an emptying of ourselves to a greater extent. And this is
indeed a blessing from God. But we do not receive
this gift unless our own gratuitous act in prayer is
offered in a pure manner, empty of a desire for self.
What our soul receives then is a stretching of our
desire toward a more complete giving away of ourselves, a release from self. A great purity of intention is constantly needed for this. For it entails the
abnegation not to receive anything *except* a greater
desire to give ourselves away. This must be a pure
desire not to receive anything except the emptying
of self. To arrive at wanting nothing for ourselves,

with no thought of a return for any giving—this emptying of self is what ultimately draws our soul more deeply into God.

~

We must learn not to savor too much the prospect of giving any gift to God before we arrive finally at giving it. The anticipation of giving can lead us to think that any gift is really ours to give. We must realize instead that we have nothing that is our exclusive possession. It is an illusion, even in offering ourselves to God, to imagine that we are making a gift to God of something that does not already belong to him. We have to remember, then, not to satisfy ourselves in giving to God, which is what we do when we think it is *our* gift, our possession, we are giving. What we seem to possess is in truth what we have only received for the sake of making it a gift. Nothing of our lives was ever exclusively ours alone. Everything we seem to possess, everything we call our own, always carries secretly within it the demand for an eventual return to God. The need to offer to God everything in our lives is a serious requirement of love clearly stated in the Gospel. But the real challenge is to offer all our mind, our heart, our soul, our strength, as though we are only rightly returning all to him who has given to us. In this sense, truly everything in our lives is on loan and needs to be offered back to God.

~

Perhaps our life at the end will be measured before God by those things we determined were impossible to relinquish despite the divine request to let go and release them. This capacity to withhold what should be given away if we are to advance in love can be an unfortunate strength acquired over a lifetime. When the awareness in our soul is strong that God is asking for anything, and a refusal wins the day, we lose almost immediately a deeper sensitivity toward God. It is as though a wall had been erected in a single day between his presence and our soul. A separation occurs, and if not overcome, a more impersonal mode of relating to God takes hold. The result is a reluctance to listen in daily life to the silent appeal of God inviting our generosity. An earlier sensitivity to God we may have enjoyed is replaced by an inclination to limit ourselves to predictable obligations toward God. Commands and orders are all we desire now to know. Nothing more may be sought. But duty fulfilled without a greater longing to please God crushes a recognition that is possible in the midst of events. More often than we think, God may be asking a question in the midst of a day's strain and irritations: "Will you lay down your life for me?" (Jn 13:38). Many times that question is whispered while facing some encounter with a poor person. If we do not realize he waits for our answer even in small sacrifices toward the poor, we soon forfeit the path toward a deeper love for God.

～

Sometimes we have to give away by an interior act of stripping and divestment what has already been taken from us without our chance to resist. The loss becomes suddenly different after we make this voluntary act of dispossession. Before that, it is difficult to avoid distress at any loss, especially when it comes unexpectedly, as though we had been robbed. Until we overcome that thought, our appreciation for sacrifice may remain at a much lower level. We forget perhaps that sacrifice requires not only what we can give away from our possession. It includes as well the offering of what has been already taken, for often we must relinquish in sacrifice what still clings to our heart. The willing surrender of what seems to have been confiscated from us, torn from us, what is no longer ours to claim, and yet what we can now release in an act of offering, leads to a blessed recognition of the passing nature of all things in our life. Sacrifice is lived more in love only as this truth deepens. We have sometimes nothing better, nothing more pleasing to God, than to offer to him what he has already taken from us.

∼

It is a spiritual image worth pondering that dates from the time of the desert fathers: to make a voluntary donation to a thief of an item he has overlooked in the course of his theft. In the account from the desert fathers, the thief, when about to depart the monk's humble dwelling, is called back and offered a hand-woven basket he might have stolen had he noticed it. The thief who has appropriated what he has no right to take is now offered as a gift an item he might earlier have stolen. But instead of stealing it, he must now receive it as a free offering. He must take it, not as an addition to the spoils of his forcible theft, but as a gift. In the account, the thief does not consider a possible refusal and walks away with the basket. And what happens? Once he begins to walk away, the effect on the thief is to shock him. Received as a gift, instead of stolen, the basket transforms all he has taken into a shameful act. He retraces his steps and returns the few objects of value he has stolen. It is not so much shame, perhaps, that overcomes the thief, but something else. He has been overwhelmed by the sight of the monk who has called happily after him down the road to make sure he does not miss the forgotten basket. With the presence of that happy monk's face lingering in his awareness, the thief loses all desire for what he has taken. When he realizes the apparent blessing he has extended to the monk by emptying him of his belongings, what value can the things he holds in his bag now have?

~

Perhaps we are not so conscious of a spiritual gift until it disappears. The loss awakens the realization of a blessing no longer enjoyed. And yet the sense of loss may be the superior grace and better than the possession of a gift we may have taken for granted. The experience of loss can provoke our soul to a greater longing, not for the return of the same gift, which may not be possible, but to be more faithful to God and all he chooses for us. The path to every deeper offering of ourselves to God passes through such experiences of loss and emptiness. The pattern is almost predictable after a while. The gifts we receive from God are often not understood until we have them no more. The experience is most poignant and painful in the people we have loved. But the experience of all things in this life departing from us in due time, including the souls we have loved, must also be anticipated. The deprivation of a gift once enjoyed can intensify our desire for the gift of God himself. The permanence of God in our lives surpasses as an ultimate gift all things that are passing away in this life.

～

"Do not aim too high, and you will not be disappointed", it is sometimes said. Even at first hearing, the words ring with a jarring cynicism. If taken seriously, they would undermine any ambitious pursuit in life. But in the spiritual realm, this sentiment is not uncommon and even identified with a semblance of humility. It may not be phrased in the same words, but the attitude is identical. It translates into a refusal to aspire to any greatness of soul. It is not just that holiness is spurned as a pursuit too demanding. The thought is that a holy life, at least for oneself, is unrealistic. It is fine to admire holiness from a distance, but to seek it as a personal goal in life would only invite frustration. Best, then, to keep to a modest approach, pacing oneself in virtue, taking care not to impose too much on oneself. What is not admitted is the lack of courage in this attitude and an essential turning away from God. For what is really declined is God's own desire to draw closer to our soul. We prefer to keep our distance from him, out of reach from his demands. We opt to refuse the gift of ourselves. There will be more regret for this basic refusal at the end of a life than for any pursuit of God that somehow falls short. For there really is no ultimate failure when a soul sincerely seeks God, even when an entire life is a perpetual struggle for God and never seems to get very far. God sees with eyes that are different from ours. And failing to become a saint is not a mark of opprobrium. A refusal to seek at all may be, however, most regrettable.

~

Real spirituality has nothing to do with the mere *idea* of holiness. And this is perhaps the total content of a first determination to seek God and a holy life. The early grace is primarily in the imaginable possibility of holiness. Time goes on, and so often only a modified resemblance to a holy life ensues. Some tempering, some fading, some merging of mixed tendencies sets in. One day fervor and the next day an indifference, a struggle for virtue followed by careless and avoidable failure. What we commonly call a good life often displays inconsistent efforts. This is not simply human weakness in triumph. Rather, more likely, a crucial moment is not faced, a threshold that must be passed if holiness is to shift from a well-meaning aspiration to a passion of the soul. God has his unique way of bringing a soul through events and interior challenges to this threshold. But in every case, it is essentially the same test, namely, to make at some point a definitive, irreversible surrender of our soul to God. We have to perceive an imperative need at this hour, on this day or night, to place our entire destiny, the whole of our life, in the hands of God, come what may. We have to see this act as ultimate and decisive, allowing no subsequent turning back or refusal. The only other option would be to run from God.

~

The giving of God to us from a timeless eternity is beyond our comprehension. But this does not excuse the fact that many acts of his kindness to us are overlooked and simply missed. They do not capture our immediate attention. Yet gifts by their very nature demand an attentiveness in order to receive them properly and not only gratitude after we recognize them. Many gifts, even those exchanged between friends, require our notice if we are not to wound the giver with an apparent indifference to the gift. The only way we will usually give a gift in return is after this recognition. Gratitude happens first in the attentiveness to a gift, and it is this attention that often draws love for the giver. This requirement of attentiveness in order to love is as true with God as it is in human relations.

~

Poverty will be perceived as a gift, and not simply a sacrifice, greater indeed than any possession, only after the "pouring out". We can see this truth in Mary of Bethany bestowing all her precious ointment on Jesus seated at table. Again, she is certainly complete in her gesture, holding back nothing, a sign always of great love. It is not a part of the jar she shares, but she breaks it entirely open. She shatters it in order to pour out all her perfume upon Jesus. Nothing is held back, no drop is kept in reserve. The house is filled with the fragrance, because the perfume is no longer hers; it has ceased any longer to belong to her as a personal possession. The excess of this gesture, its extravagance, expresses the essential truth about love. Neither love nor the perfume, in this case, can remain enclosed in a container, protected and saved. Instead, it must be all thrown away in the hour of love, wasted imprudently without a thought for tomorrow, poured out in its entirety. If she was not so poor before this gesture, Mary of Bethany became poor afterward. The poverty here is inseparable from great love, which requires extravagant gestures of this sort, lest it settle for a lesser degree of love.

～

Every heroic spiritual life finishes in some form of crucifixion, and typically a crucifixion concealed

from the eyes of others. This would seem abso-
lutely inevitable in the spiritual realm. The soul
more united to God cannot avoid its own passion
in the last period of life. There seems to be no option, no variation on this spiritual truth. The conclusion of a holy life culminates in a final offering
that has been preparing itself for a long time. This
last offering may have a largely unseen quality, but
certainly it is real for the soul. Some souls clearly
recognize this share in the Passion of Christ and
never lose this awareness, while some suffer confusion. God is never so predictable; even at the end
of lives, he can surprise and shock. But in all these
souls, there is a completion of a gift of themselves.
For many years they have been offering to him.
And now they have no greater mark of their simplicity and effacement before God than a constant
and essential prayer to exhaust all things in themselves for him.

7

The Import of Contemplative Surrenders

"All knowledge of Him is but a kind of recognition. The true way of knowing God is to suffer oneself to be known by Him."

—Charles Journet

"We only 'seize' God, in a manner of speaking, after we have been 'seized' by him."

—Henri de Lubac, S.J.

"I am not asking you so much to gaze upon Christ during your prayer of contemplation as to become aware of the fact that he does not for a moment cease to gaze upon you."

—Saint Teresa of Avila

The spiritual hunger of the contemplative can be satisfied only by a full surrender of the soul to God. The longing of a contemplative soul finds its completion precisely in this deeper offering and surrender to God. The manner in which God draws this surrender in prayer is a mysterious

*aspect of each contemplative life. It has its unique varia-
tions in each life, but one essential fact is that a complete
surrender of the soul is demanded by the nature of love.
The need to offer all to God becomes a dominant urge
within the soul of the contemplative and, indeed, within
prayer itself. God in turn seems to find circumstances in
which the contemplative soul is faced with this need as the
only manner in which it can live out its hunger for God.
The surrender that takes place in prayer is often simply a
response to what God has shown as an exclusive option
for a soul if it is to plunge ahead in its relations of absolute
love for God.*

It is of interest certainly to peruse the instructions
on the transitional periods of spiritual life that can
be found in treatise form in the Catholic tradition,
much of it descriptive of symptoms to expect if we
advance in prayer. But perhaps more important to
recognize is the need for acts of radical surrender
to God that do not fit so easily on a roadmap.
The junctures in life in which God seeks a blind,
trusting surrender to himself are not so predictable
and often not identified until they suddenly confront us. But perhaps they are perceived more frequently when we place a high premium on letting
God take from us what we might easily refuse to
give him. These can be smaller things, satisfactions
in work, friendships, attachments, but sometimes
greater, such as our health or the loss of someone

much loved in our lives. In prayerful surrenders of this sort, small or great, we allow God to gain victories over us. We release our natural grip on possessiveness, our clinging to passing things that are bound to disappear eventually from our lives. We have to learn at times not to defend ourselves against these losses when they come. There is a blessedness in being defeated when the one who vanquishes is God himself. It is true that we may never get used to losing in this manner and may never find it pleasant. Yet these losses are not without compensation. The readiness to "give what he takes and take what he gives", as Mother Teresa often repeated, becomes a measure of our soul. Always the impulse to lay down our life means another step closer to him and, ultimately, a step nearer to the mystery of his own surrender on the Cross.

〜

One of the lessons prayer teaches after a time is the impossibility of a quest for God directed and shaped by our own devices. There is no "managing" our relations with God. No effort of our own can draw our soul nearer to God. The best we can do at times is to cultivate a receptivity to God, an accessibility open to his silent advances—and then wait upon his initiatives. There is, however, an insight in prayer that opens our soul to the greater discovery. The leap comes in realizing that God *wants* nothing but complete surrender, although he will never make an absolute demand for it. This recognition begins to invite us, gently at first, but then with insistence, drawing us strongly so that our silence in prayer begins to be filled with that desire. The act of unreserved surrender to God after a certain point becomes then a true leap. It can be called one of those points of no return in prayer. In a certain sense, if we persevere in this surrender to God, we relinquish all our tendency to retain an independence from God. There is nothing more desirable now than to let our soul be entirely subject to God.

$\sim$

"Give God permission", Mother Teresa used to say, as she did to Cardinal John O'Connor, the former Archbishop of New York, in her first words to him on the day he was ordained a bishop by Pope Saint John Paul II at Saint Peter's in Rome. If in prayer we pronounce a very direct and explicit "yes" to God, we allow him to draw us closer to himself. But we may not find what we initially expect. He is likely to contradict what we anticipate. It is not just foolish expectations that he will frustrate. As a result of that prayer, the Cross may become a more frequent companion in our lives and, along with the Cross, an experience of a greater concealment in God. The concealment is not at all a rejection or estrangement or a permanent distance from God that we simply have to bear through life. We will find that God's concealment is actually a game of hiding that he invites us to enter. It is not a competitive game with a winner and loser in a strict sense. But it is a game that does have its rules. We can become a player in this game of God's hiding only by forsaking all prognostications or predictions of what he will do. Again, this game is not a competition involving a contest between opponents in which a struggle for victory takes place. The game requires, instead, that we allow another to triumph over and over again. What may seem a defeat at times is really not at all a loss. The apparent defeat is to allow God to lead in determining what is to come. We have given God permission to indicate what pleases him. We must now give ourselves in surrender to what he shows is his choice and offer ourselves to his choice. What we might prefer instead will then gradually disappear from our desire, but this is not a loss. The triumph of God becomes also our own, a conquering of ourselves, as we surrender the desire to retain possession of our own choices.

~

The notion of progress in contemplation is perhaps not a helpful idea. Contemplatives themselves say they never advance very far, certainly not in any type of heightened perception. But of course "seeing" is not the primary point in contemplation, despite the suggestion in the word of a more penetrating quality of sight. It is love that is the great aim in contemplative lives; all else is secondary. If there is wisdom or deeper insight in them, it is due to love and the union with God that love fosters, a union just as likely to bring blindness and an absence of perception as it is to provide rich insights. Can it be said, then, that contemplatives nonetheless seek something definite and concrete in a spiritual sense, something that can offer a measure of progress? The answer can only be an indirect one. Every true contemplative certainly desires a release from self, a giving away of self, an unshackling of attachment to self, in order to enter more freely into God's love. This effort may offer some measure of progress, but it is not in any sense a final goal. It provides only the accompaniment to the grace of contemplation. The real goal cannot be measured, for the contemplative's life depends ultimately on an increasing, limitless surrender to God. In that deeper realm of soul, the contemplative life of surrender is a pursuit without an identifiable target. These souls accept to walk a pilgrimage of endless departures for a destination that is never really known. They are on a journey without clear markers, seeking only to disappear by the surrender of love into the immeasurable presence of another's love.

~

An essential property of love, according to Saint Thomas Aquinas, is to be ecstatic—not in the crude sense of raw, sensual emotion, but as a spiritual force tearing a person out of self. Every real love causes a rupture in the interior life of a soul, a rending within the soul, in which the inner self is seized and divided and left for some time without a way back to itself. In one sense, this rupture is a release from self. The soul can find no peace alone with self and casts about in searching for its love, consumed with desire for the beloved. In another sense, the rupture means an entrapment of the soul within itself, the soul unable to escape a painful inward deprivation in the absence of the beloved. This tearing of the heart in love invites a recognition about the nature of love, usually early in a life. A discovery has to be made. The initial experience of the violence inflicted on the heart by love determines for some people whether they will love selflessly or love largely for the sake of what they can receive in love. A pure choice for love itself must take place, or else love in its genuine truth may never be sought as the great aspiration in life. It will instead fade and die a natural death. This pure choice for love entails a great surrender to being wounded by love and not turning back. Few who make this discovery are likely to lead ordinary spiritual lives.

~

An effort to overcome the pain of not loving adequately can be a misdirected endeavor. It is not the pain of love that is a problem. For we cannot love without at times the humiliating experience of failing in love. We come up short in love as part of the very nature of love. If instead we should find ourselves at some point enjoying a sense of achievement in love, it would mean we have embraced an illusion. The true measure of love is to know our deficiency in love. This is a sign ordinarily that our effort to love is plunging into concrete actions and is not confined to an abstract notion. Without concrete exertion, it is always possible to deceive ourselves that we love sufficiently. A needed question can protect us from this deception. Can we ever love enough when the love we have received infinitely exceeds our least recognition? The thought may leave us dissatisfied and yet ready to stretch ourselves in greater self-giving.

~

"Intense love does not measure; it just gives" (Mother Teresa). The heart has to give itself away to God in prayer. This is the nature of love, that someone sought in love seizes all from us and draws our gift of self in a complete manner. A surrender to God of all we possess, of all that we might hold back from him, is an essential requirement in the deeper path of prayer. It is the essential act in love. There is nothing in that act that implies a later restoration of what has been surrendered. To offer all in love is to risk having all taken from us. We should not expect some form of reappropriation that will return what has been given away. In some cases, indeed, the offering of all to God in surrender will be irreversible. There will be no turning back. All the more should we make such acts with an absolute seriousness of soul. The most we can anticipate with certainty in a prayer of great surrender is that God will give himself in return for every loss we seem to experience in subsequent days.

～

There can be a vast difference in prayer between the words we speak and the actual request implicit in those words. We do not know sometimes what we are asking in prayer. It remains for God to show us over time the true significance of the words we have used. Even when the words we speak are sincere and seem clear in our own understanding, there remains the possibility of a great unknown fulfillment of the prayer we have made of which only God knows. How will God respond, for instance, when in our prayer we open ourselves completely to his entry into our life? How will he complete our sincere offering to him? The answer to such a prayer is never identical to the spiritual expectation explicitly expressed in the prayer. God may be listening to the implicit request that has a source in the unseen depth of our soul. We know this because God's way of answering our prayer seems often to mean some greater taste of the Cross. This eventuality, while perhaps acknowledged somewhat by our soul, is a truth awaiting its completion. But this means in turn that we should understand that we have prayed for more than we can sometimes realize at that time.

～

Every act of surrender to God of lasting spiritual value takes place in a silence deep within ourselves. We must make this surrender of ourselves to God from a depth of silence that we cannot really perceive even in prayer but that is always present in our soul. It is, as well, the same unseen depth where every cross extended to us must be embraced. In that sense, the act of surrender and the cross are united. We must make this surrender in prayer without knowing indeed what cross in the days ahead it may bring to our lives. The willingness to surrender is all God asks for the moment. The surrender alone at the present time is necessary. Without this act of surrender, however, we have no proper sense of an offering still waiting to be revealed in our lives. But with it Our Lord prepares us and eventually makes known the greater offering he wants. He himself will be encountered in a more personal manner as we continue to surrender to him. That deeper realm within our soul where these surrenders take place becomes a place of real contact with him precisely as he offers us the Cross. There we recognize implicitly that our surrender to him has a real link to his Passion in a mysterious manner. We can sense that he desires now to share this truth with us and will make this discovery more evident to us.

~

It is certainly true that no deeper relations with God can persist unless a surrender of ourselves takes place again and again in silence. A silence within ourselves must be entered that may appear at first to be an inner desolation and a lost way. Nonetheless, we must enter this interior realm of emptiness where the intrusion of egoism no longer is an obstacle. The silence there can seem vast, as though we

were gazing across a stretch of desert with no option but to proceed ahead. Our soul must forget itself in turning now to God. And it must not give in
to any hesitation. It may seem that we have entered
a dark, directionless path from which there may be
no destination. But this is a mistaken thought and a
semblance of intimidation that must be conquered.
Our soul has at that point not yet made the deeper
surrender that brings a light to the blindness that
may have overtaken us temporarily. The surrender
to God will bring a new taste in this silence. The
presence that our soul is still unable to touch or
gaze upon will be known as strangely near. And
that is always enough.

~

Confusion between feeling and the will in the life
of prayer can produce the illusion that strong feelings are identical to resolute interior choices. But
strong passion, even toward God, is not a sign that
we have chosen anything yet with a strong will,
only that we have been animated and inflamed with
desire. A choice for a more complete surrender to
God, for instance, is distinct from the mere attraction to this aspiration. It is the interior choice for
God, as an utterly free, unconditional offering, and
not simply the desire for God, as strong as this may
be, that must be exercised with regularity in prayer.

Sometimes such an interior choice can ride, as it were, on the current of strong feeling. But more often there is no support from any passionate feeling. The will finds itself unaccompanied by feelings and even heavy in its absence of feeling. Yet it is good to recall that a layer of desire resides in the soul far beneath emotion, ready to inflame the will even without feeling. The determined choice to give ourselves to God can reach into the dry and silent depths of our human soul. It happens simply by offering ourselves again to all that is the current choice of God in our lives.

∽

"God is the soul of our soul", writes Saint John of the Cross. But this image ought not to be interpreted too literally. The divine indwelling does not occur spatially within the soul's inner regions, as though God could be confined in a secret place inside our soul. It is perhaps more accurate and fruitful to say that God dwells within our soul's act of surrender to him. The intensity of a surrender to God at the center of our soul will always correspond in a certain manner to the intensity of divine love inhabiting the soul. Surrender implies a profound renunciation of ourselves and a complete offering of ourselves. The Lord enters inside this internal state of self-offering and remains there as in his own home. His presence unites itself with the act of our soul's surrender to him. Our soul's offering of itself in a complete gift makes our soul porous and accessible to the flow of God's contact. This openness to God intensifies as long as a deep surrender permeates the innermost desires of our soul.

～

The power of God to draw us in love can be said to depend in part on our human response. This acknowledges a preference in God not to exercise the full extent of his power. He has chosen not to overwhelm us with his love if that would mean we have no choice to refuse. And yet our human freedom may not actually be so strong in resisting divine love. Once we invite God more fully into our lives, the semblance of strength we earlier possessed to remain more distant and detached from him is lost. A serious act of offering ourselves to God has this consequence. Henceforth we are no longer able to control the divine flame and prevent it from burning us. Even in the natural experience of human love, can a person in love temper and regulate the feelings that surge in the heart? No more, then, can a soul that crosses a threshold in love for God now tamp down and control the fire by which God draws it. The power of God to love is waiting to be unleashed upon a soul, which sometimes requires only a single passionate word spoken from us in silence. God takes us at our word when it is spoken from some depth, and if we offer ourselves completely to him, his love may burn our soul in extreme ways beyond our capacity to resist. But who after crossing such a threshold has ever found a reason to regret this result or asked that it cease?

⁓

Sometimes this act of offering involves events that overcome us unexpectedly and bring trial and difficulty. After the fact, when an event is finished and a loss is now felt, an offering to God can be made. But more subtly such an offering should be directed to the satisfactions that seem to come and go in the interior life of prayer. When satisfaction disappears from prayer and we are struggling with obscurity and inner emptiness, we should not wait to make an offering. The loss of comfort in prayer is an opportunity to give away what we no longer enjoy. What is meant is not just a disciplined refusal to demand back for the interior life what has now passed. Rather, an offering to God of what is now no longer can be concretely made. And it serves to place us in greater detachment from ourselves out of love of him.

⁓

The real meaning of spirituality as a life fully *engaged* with God may begin in earnest at the hour when our soul adamantly refuses to take flight from God. Perhaps we realize intuitively then that our soul is on the verge of unknown, costly consequences in seeking closeness to God. But if we refuse to back-track and continue to offer ourselves to God, the courage of that hour can mark the rest of a life. Perhaps before this we are simply playing with the idea of spirituality and prayer, treating them in the same way we might look with admiration at a painting of some beauty that we keep moving to various locations inside a room. We like to have it for an occasional view, but never desire to gaze at it for too long. In contrast, there is no more occasional attention to God after our soul crosses a certain threshold of offering itself to God. The yearning to make a gift to God of one's soul becomes then a steady contemplative hunger that returns in some manner every day in prayer.

∽

If a soul becomes genuinely contemplative, a deeper desire within it converges more and more upon a single need: to give itself in a complete offering to God. Only in that act can our soul discover a way to assuage the increasing taste of poverty within itself. The poverty as it intensifies seems to assert an absence of any possession that might be offered to God. And, indeed, it is true that our soul has nothing it can take as its own and extend to God as a gift. There is only one gift that can be made, and that is a complete offering of ourselves in love. The irony in this is that the poverty of the contemplative, the emptiness that fills our soul when poverty is realized more sharply, becomes the only acceptable offering we can make to God. A complete offering of our poverty must now sustain us in prayer. The nothingness we have come to know within ourselves must be offered back completely to God. This offering is the one yearning that can drive and impel all our desires—to make a complete gift to God of our own poverty and nothingness.

8

The Allure of Silence

"The word has resonance when you hear the silence in it, when it hides and leaves you to guess its treasure, which it releases bit by bit, without haste and frivolous agitation. Silence is the secret ingredient in the words that count. The value of a soul is found in its silences."

—Antonin Sertillanges, O.P.

"When one speaks with love of God, all human words are like lions become blind, seeking a watering place in the desert."

—Léon Bloy

"A long speech is one thing, a long love another."

—Saint Augustine

Silence is loved by every soul hungry for a deeper life of prayer. It is natural to a prayerful soul to experience a need for silence and for time alone with God. This attraction draws the soul even when silence can become a difficult trial due to distraction or anxieties. But silence is also a school of learning in the relations of our soul with God. It proves its worth in the longer experience of prayer. The silence of the soul in spending time before a tabernacle in the presence of the Lord becomes a sacred mystery over time. For many people, this commitment to silence in prayer becomes an essential part of their life. They can no more live without silence in a church or chapel than live without a heart that can feel and respond to other men. It may be that silence does not immediately attract us. It can therefore be helpful to know what silence brings to the time of prayer.

The Gospel scenes on the lake of Galilee are often dramatic, but surely not everything has been written down. Perhaps lessons on prayer also took place out on that lake. And what instructions on prayer might Jesus have taught in a fishing boat lapped by waves in the middle of a large lake far from the shore? He may have told his apostles not to be anxious for a return to the shore once out on the lake or to leave prayer so easily. Once out on the water, a soul of prayer should not want to return too quickly to the shore and should only do so with some regret. He may have also told his apostles not to be concerned in prayer for arriving at a destination; rather, to let the boat drift with the tide when far from the shore. He may have told them that rowing with rigor in a direction we determine is necessary at times, but it is not good as a regular exercise in prayer. We must allow the boat to meander somewhat in the breezes and thereby enjoy the free movement of the deeper water carrying the boat. He may have encouraged them to seek the sunsets on the water and the silence of light shimmering in a streak of red on the water. He may have told them to love quiet when they pray and to listen in prayer as one can listen to the rhythm of waves beating gently against the wooden sides of a boat.

∼

In prayer our attraction to silence corresponds ordinarily to our desire to love. Inasmuch as the desire to love permeates our awareness more strongly, our mind wants to think less. This link between silence and love is a grace and not something we can achieve by effort. Moreover, the greater desire to love while in silence before God is not something that any thought in itself can perceive. It is an attraction within our soul's depth. The manner in which silence accompanies this inner desire to love shows varying patterns. There can be a desire to love that is a frustrated longing and a dry emptiness felt within ourselves. Silence then is often troubled and difficult to maintain. There can be as well a desire to love by giving away ourselves in an offering, and then the sense of a deeper silence within our soul continues as long as the desire to give of ourselves remains. There is a desire to love with a clarity fixed on the one loved, and the silence in our soul tends then to be more complete. And there is a silence filled by the desire simply to love more, to discover in love a more complete release from ourselves. At that time the silence within us becomes in itself an absence of thought about ourselves. The more complete it is, the more it is savored as a stimulus to the greater surrender of our soul to God.

∼

It can be said that prayer in the silence of a church or chapel starts well by striving for a turn toward Someone other than self—someone whom we adore and love. From the first minutes of prayer, the Lord must be sought as a real existence near in his presence to our own soul in the immediate hour. This can be done only in a deep conviction of faith. And of course this conviction is made easier when we are praying in a chapel or church before the Blessed Sacrament. At the same time, the Lord must be sought with an implicit recognition that the reality of his presence does not depend on the satisfaction of an encounter with him. Satisfying or not, the encounter with him is a reality and begins as we prostrate ourselves in love before his person. We do not need to seek feelings of his presence, as though they are required for prayer. His presence in silence is already real, and the conversation of one heart with another is ready to begin simply by the first word spoken. We begin well, then, by rousing again our conviction of faith and bringing ourselves to the existing personal presence unseen before our blind eyes. Placing our love as a humble gift before the presence of the Lord in a tabernacle, we are ready to enter receptively into the contemplative encounter with God. There will be no need to concern ourselves with our experience of this encounter. The reality of his presence is enough to sustain all we seek in the depth of our heart.

～

There is a need in the silence of prayer to share ourselves with God—to be communicative, not closed up or withdrawn. Our soul wants this communication with God, this release of our deeper desires from their captive and inchoate state. In this effort, we need not be eloquent in the language we use, for no choice of words is really ever adequate to express the deeper desires of the soul. Nonetheless, we must express desire in prayer, sometimes in great simplicity and even without words, perhaps most of all when silence permeates our prayer and desire has no language to translate it. It is always from a deeper desire for God that we must seek the expression that is fitting for that day. Prayer emerges from our heart's innermost desire, sometimes with an outpouring of words and other times with hardly any word. On the other hand, prayer that fails to communicate desire for God cannot really be prayer; it can only be some form of interior numbness or a turn upon ourselves. It may be only then a desire for ourselves that is concealed beneath words. But this should not be. We have only to direct our gaze again toward a tabernacle to allow our soul's yearning to be rekindled toward the Lord's invisible gaze. And then we learn once again to long for him in the language of desire.

∽

In loving God while in silent prayer, a tension sometimes arises in us between what can be expressed in words and an inexpressible realm of desire in our soul that finds no adequate words and remains inarticulate. At first this realm of muted desire seems a reason for frustration. It seems wrong that the inner passion of our soul should be incapable of a release in words. But then we make the discovery that our soul's inmost desire actually has its own language, a language known quite well to God. It is a language not capable of translation into familiar words. The impossibility of translation turns out, however, to be fine and acceptable. We discover that there is no need to seek words when this language of desire is speaking in our heart. At some point, our soul understands that God comprehends this language perfectly. And once we understand this truth, we perceive that he himself begins to speak this same language of longing more frequently to our soul.

∼

For anyone who prays with deeper faith, the personal presence of God will be certain and constant, especially in praying quietly before a tabernacle or monstrance. But knowing that Our Lord is present in a church or chapel does not mean that prayer brings satisfaction. The certainty of his presence may be unquestionable. But of course he does not show his face or speak clear words. Our incapacity for a more tangible contact in silent prayer can carve a loneliness into our soul precisely when we are seeking the company of his presence. But we are never alone in prayer, and faith can teach us over time a different manner of contact with the presence of God. The difference between what our senses would like to enjoy in love and what our spirit requires has to be reconciled. This tension indeed comes to be recognized as an experience of love itself. Our Lord will in fact reveal his personal presence inasmuch as he draws longing from our soul. The return of a deeper longing for God within the soul is his way of speaking to our soul. It is his language of love for us in the time of silence. He bestows this longing as his personal gift. If our soul does not resist and allows divine love to take the lead in love, we learn that deeper love for God has some link always to this longing. The lack of satiation in our soul's experience of love, the absence of enjoyment over long stretches of time, can disappear as a matter of concern. Our soul is left only with its never diminished longing and the power of love it conceals.

~

The failure to be receptive in silence to the reality of a revealed Christian truth usually means that we do not grow in contemplative faith. A realization of the truth of the real presence of Christ in the Eucharist, for example, requires such a silence in our soul and a hunger of soul for the Lord that intensifies only in silence. The truth of Jesus' bodily presence in a chapel or church does not respond to an analytical effort. There is no act of unraveling or deciphering this truth, no evidence by which to decode the mystery. Nothing tangible supports the act of faith in gazing on a monstrance during Eucharistic adoration. We can know by faith with a conviction of indisputable surety that he is there in the immediacy of his presence. But a silence of the soul is required for the deeper interiority of this conviction. The yearning of the soul for a reality that defies the experience of the senses demands this silence. Indeed, there can be no deeper awareness of Our Lord's real presence without this silence. The silence is typically a state of subdued awe at being in the invisible presence of God himself.

~

"It is a sealed fountain that does not communicate to a stranger" (Saint Bernard). Perhaps we do not realize enough how much we must protect the *personal* dimension of our soul's exchange with God. Prayer is a response to a real person, not simply an exercise of piety making use of words and religious sentiments. It is an act of reciprocation toward someone who has extended his hand to us, inviting us to draw closer. In a very personal way, we must be ready to receive from him and to give to him. All this is very personal, and like all real relations with a person it is new each time that we turn to prayer. Nonetheless, this personal dimension of prayer does not always come easily. The main reason for difficulty is that, after a certain point, prayer requires an entry into a deeper silence within the soul where any encounter with God must take place. This silence is the location of every deeper contact with his personal presence. The greater mystery of God is met there.

~

Nonetheless, the silence that sometimes hides him and encloses him can seem limitless, forbidding, intimidating in its depth. The silence can seem to have an impersonal quality. In longer periods of silence, we face more defenselessly the real mystery of God, which earlier in our lives may have been simply a truth to be pondered. At times in silence, it can be easy to think that God is not present at all, at least as someone who is personally with us. We may simply feel very alone, with no way to release ourselves from this condition. But the sense of affliction is deceiving. The great truth is that God hides in that silence, however blinding and beclouding it seems to be. His gaze upon the depth of our soul is steady and secure. His look upon our soul is indeed inexhaustible in its love. But we must remember that it reaches down to depths within our soul that we cannot perceive. This gaze of divine love is itself a primary mystery received in prayer, no matter what we experience of emptiness or incomprehension. We simply have to hold firmly to the personal presence of God near us, within us. Once we realize this sacred truth, nothing should shake us from this firm conviction. There is no loss of his presence any longer from one time of prayer to another. The presence of his eyes rests upon our soul permanently.

~

Our mind's natural restlessness does not always take easily to silence. By a natural disinclination, our mind will at times resist silence and an absence of thought. Remaining empty of thought in a complete silence seems to our natural state of mind a wasteful, undesirable condition. Yet contemplative life demands this silencing of the mind—as long as it is not artificially induced. The mind in prayer has to learn that there is a deeper attentiveness to God in silence that does not need thoughts to occupy it. The mind at such a time has to guard itself against a single obstacle, namely, turning its thought and concentration toward self. Such a propensity, if not conquered, will turn prayer into self-conscious introspection. Reflexive tendencies, when they dominate, are contrary to the grace of prayer and must be disciplined and overcome. The great need in the silence of prayer is to lean away from self and turn a loving attention toward God.

~

Our mind in silent prayer is properly oriented when it is receptive to an intuitive act. This is in contrast to thought that would labor in analysis, seeking answers or a clear understanding. Sometimes, of course, a reflective pondering in prayer is necessary and beneficial. But this is not always the better option in silent prayer. There are spiritual insights received only in silence when the flow of our thought is temporarily suspended, and we simply wait upon God in a wordless longing. When it happens, we must not leave that longing but, rather, enter the silence of it fully, letting ourselves be drawn into its attraction. The choice to remain in waiting and not to depart from this silencing of thought often determines the deeper fruitfulness of prayer. This choice does not require strenuous effort, nor is it something we choose in a forced manner. The silence itself will attract us and draw us to the quieting of thought. Prayer at that point can be like listening for the stirring of wind in nearby trees that we expect soon to arrive but do not yet hear, waiting for the leaves to rustle before the cool breeze is felt on our face.

~

"He who possesses in truth the word of Jesus can hear even its silence" (Saint Ignatius of Antioch). To listen in silence with our attention fixed on nothing but a desire for God is not to wait for his words, not to hear him speak in that hour of prayer, certainly not in words that communicate a clear message. This listening is not directed to hearing any words. Yet it is an openness to receiving a communication. The silence allows our soul to encounter a real language, but it is not a language of words. It is spoken through a vehicle of longing and desire. The soul is intent on listening in order to receive a communication not dependent on words. God speaks to the attentive soul in a single word, a word not heard in a voice or found in the dictionary but buried in a desire beneath hearing. And our soul can come to know this word resonating in its own depth. God expresses quite clearly at times his longing to our soul for its offering and its return of love. The listening of our soul in prayer is not to hear a voice making this request but to recognize a mysterious and sacred presence asking for this return of love. Our soul knows then that it is known in love to God, and the soul knows itself as loving in return. The listening in the silence of prayer is directed primarily to this truth of being known in love and of responding in turn with longing.

～

Silence is an essential condition for receptivity in prayer to God. The silence is not God, of course, but he uses it to communicate his real presence in mystery to the soul. But our soul must leave itself accessible and open to his mysterious language of silent love during that time. The silence, when it is empty of thought, intensifies a longing for God. This yearning for God felt deep in the soul is precisely God's way of communicating to our soul his own personal love. The soul seems to diminish in importance as its yearning for God intensifies. It is empty of itself in that silence. To some degree or other, the silence seems to convey a certitude of God and his presence. He is there in silence, drawing our soul to a longing for him. Our mind does not need to think in any active manner; indeed, it has no desire to take up any thoughts, no need to hear a message or instruction. The silence is sufficient, just as the company of a loved one is enough even when no words are exchanged. There is simply no need in this depth of silent prayer to seek for a communication by words. The soul already has its assurance of the love it is experiencing. It is present in the longing for God that permeates it.

~

On some calm days in prayer there may be a silence that drifts with ease into our soul and that seems to make an encounter with God a perfectly natural experience. But it may not lead so readily to a graced time of prayer. Sometimes the silence enjoyed in prayer can be seductive. It becomes its own pursuit. The enjoyment of it becomes a kind of indulged act, with less attention to God himself. There is another kind of silence on a different day that causes a strain in the soul, causing it to twist inwardly with a sense of emptiness and absence. It is the impersonal quality of this silence that above all perhaps makes it forbidding and painful. But it must not be evaded or chased away. It may conceal in its discord and opposition to the soul's immediate desire a purification that will take our soul into deeper waters. When that harder silence is lived through with love, our soul keeps the turn of its attention toward God. The painful aspect of the prayer belies an actual closeness to God that may be real. It will be likely outside the hour of prayer that this is known, in the providential opportunities for charity that quickly show their face in the immediate day.

9

Interior Deportment in Prayer

"When I try to find relief beholding You in the Sacrament, I find this greater sorrow: I cannot enjoy You wholly. All things are affliction since I do not see You as I desire, and I die because I do not die."

— Saint John of the Cross

"To anyone who loves, this truth is immediately obvious; the face and the voice of the Beloved are at each instant as new for him as though he had never yet beheld them."

— Hans Urs von Balthasar

"Man can say nothing of what he is incapable of feeling, but he can feel what he is incapable of putting into words."

— Saint Augustine

There is a kind of interior deportment of soul necessary for prayer. This is not a matter of method or strict conduct to be employed in prayer, but a certain demeanor and approach that allows the hunger of our soul to be freely and more easily aroused. There are attractions that must be cultivated, recognitions that must be returned to, favorite remembrances that can be an easy stimulus to the recovery of our love. It is customary for prayer to begin with a need to cast oil upon a flame, but we must have this oil ready at hand. The divine person of Jesus Christ will draw our soul certainly inasmuch as we allow him to be near. The notion of deportment suggests that we have to find our own way, not imitating in any strictly methodic manner an approach to prayer we have at one time learned, but making a discovery of what can commonly draw our soul more deeply into the encounter with the hidden mystery of God.

The contemplative seeks a God who keeps to his hiding, and the good contemplative does not balk at the rules of this game. But an acquired taste for the God of concealment is cause of a similar demand to conceal ourselves in hiddenness, to give up our concern for self and allow all focus on ourselves to disappear. The discovery by a contemplative that God is always beyond reach, even in his nearness, intensifies over time a desire to lose all attention on self while in prayer. As God is known more profoundly to be still hiding and unreachable, we experience a demand for a dying and giving away of self. The correspondence between the hiddenness of God tasted in prayer and a strongly felt need to die to self is always present in contemplative souls. They are inseparable realizations operating within a soul. The concealment of God cannot be experienced without urging at the same time a demand for a disappearance from ourselves. The need to strip attention from ourselves is thus a correlative to the concealment of God in his transcendent mystery. This may be why so often, in one form or another, the contemplative when praying prostrates in adoration and poverty before the absolute transcendence of God. It is a gesture of concealment to place one's face to the ground before the majesty of God.

~

It can be helpful in this regard to realize that our consciousness of self is a form of possession and, therefore, contrary to a spirit of interior poverty. We can live at times as if in a kind of personal ownership of self. Yet the identity we assume is ours may in fact be something of an illusion. This is not to suggest a Buddhist notion of an essential non-being in our identity. The point is rather to acknowledge the subtle egoistic tendency that infiltrates our prayer. It coarsens our awareness and deceives us in prayer. The instruction of Saint John of the Cross to "conceal" ourselves in prayer addresses an essential need to empty ourselves of self. There can be an inclination in us to make prayer, on the contrary, a self-seeking enterprise. We would like experiences in prayer that would prove memorable, concrete, and lasting. We would like to achieve results and leave prayer with some sense of a gratifying experience. Our tendency to seek for self is strong, even as we may deceive ourselves that this seeking is a form of love. Prayer requires a contrary inclination and a turn to greater poverty. We must abandon the self and instead direct our attention to God. This effort can be very difficult on many days. The self does not disappear so easily from importance. It is not as simple as leaving our shoes behind at the doorway of prayer. We have to forsake what clings to us in the immediate hour and attempt again to seek the eternal One whose infinite greatness is completely superior to our own small concerns.

∼

As mentioned, Saint John of the Cross insists that our soul must "conceal itself" in the time of prayer. But what exactly does he mean by this phrase, and why is it so necessary? Surely he refers to the need to turn our attention away from any preoccupation with self. The goal of prayer is to let go of ourselves and to absorb ourselves exclusively in God. The loss of self that Jesus so strikingly requires of us in the Gospel must extend in a particular manner to the hour of prayer. Indeed, the poverty of losing self must take place first in prayer. In effect, our attention must renounce the tendency to turn back upon ourselves as well as our expectation of what we might receive in prayer. This effort cannot be a rigorous exercise of concentration so much as a letting go happily of concern for self. We must replace a natural egoistic tendency with a consuming desire for God. The choice and the option after a time should be quite attractive.

~

A discomfort at the outset of prayer may be a fear that nothing is the same when we bring ourselves anew before the divine mystery. We begin not knowing whether the hour in front of us will light a flame or cast ashes upon our desires. There is no method, no sure and reliable technique, for renewing our soul's contact with God. Faith alone is our entry into the encounter with the Lord, but even faith does not determine what kind of encounter we will now have. The pure offering of our being is all we can strive for, and even this does not prevent feeling at times an inner dread of discovering in silence much more our own emptiness than God. Sometimes we may wish that prayer could simply return to the previous day and continue where we left off. But it is impossible to give ourselves to God and revert backward in time. Seeking God in silent prayer demands facing always the unpredictable experience of the present hour.

∽

Certainly it is true that our relations with God have a form of memory and accumulated experience, like all real relationships. Our prior knowledge and experience of God in prayer can be a groundwork already dug for meeting God again in a fresh manner. Nonetheless, if real communication is to occur between God and our soul, this can never be a backward turn to retrieve or reclaim a previous experience. We must give ourselves always anew to God as though doing so for the first time. Courage is necessary because the present hour of prayer may contradict everything received from the previous day. Prayer today may entail the complete absence of the comfort and nearness of God that seemed so secure one day earlier. Perhaps on such days we cannot but long for what seemed permanent the day before. Nonetheless, God clearly takes the lead here in drawing us to a greater offering. It is only in the present hour that these offerings take place, not in any return to the past. There is no such thing in prayer as living off the interest of prior investments. We have to offer ourselves *now* to God and receive as he chooses in the present day.

~

A temptation in prayer can be a desire to anchor and stabilize in some permanence our more impassioned experiences of love for God. This is a temptation that accompanies times of felt consolations in prayer. We would like our love to remain always inflamed, that a fiery love could be exercised on demand. But the experience of prayer has no absolute permanency; it is always subject to fluctuation and change. This truth, however, is not easily accepted. For some people, it is hardly possible to avoid questioning why we should be subject to such variations in our affective relations with God. It would seem so much better for love to burn with perpetual ardor. But these thoughts are an obstacle to prayer and, indeed, temptations. They impede our recognition that it is not primarily our emotion that God seeks but our deeper surrender of soul.

~

The grace of prayer is not a collector's item. It cannot be held in safekeeping, stored for later use beyond the duration of a current hour of prayer. We never simply return to yesterday's encounter with God in prayer. Indeed, no interior experience of grace in prayer of any kind is ever replicated if we mean by that a replay of what was received earlier. We have to go in a fresh manner each day to prayer, not knowing what God will provide. We can only be assured that he is present and will be listening to our soul's longing. But this must be a new longing we bring to prayer with each day.

～

This important rule of prayer is often ignored. Prayer can never be an effort to recover a previous encounter with God. With each hour of prayer alone and in silence before God, we have to open again in a fresh manner toward the divine mystery. We have to seek the eternal mystery of God anew in the present hour. Real contact with the presence of God, in other words, is not by returning to a memory. God is a reality in the immediacy of the hour at hand. The present moment is the necessary and exclusive place of encounter. Contact with him in prayer must correspond to the reality of his presence now, at this hour, on this day.

～

The desire to "re-experience" a grace that was given at one time and is now concluded misses the need to seek God anew in the current moment of life. Grace is active only in the here and now.

A memory of a grace received at one time can be fine stimulus for some action, but it is only a reminder. In that sense, the remembrance of a grace from the past may have no more vital life than a photograph of a person. It can affect us, move us to action, but it is not alive in itself in the present hour. We must seek always God in the immediacy of a current request from him.

~

Always in contemplative life, God responds in a special manner to our own inner disposition of "accessibility". And so it should be cultivated within our interior life. A receptive openness without any conditions seems to draw God's movement in love toward our soul. It is not as though an act of our soul is the cause behind a gratuitous grace. Rather, it seems that God in turn makes himself more accessible to us when we abandon ourselves fully to his choice for the present hour. Our disposition of accessibility is in effect a receptivity to his divine predilection. Before too long, however, the very accessibility to God that opened up within our soul the possibility of a more personal approach from God may open the way for the entry of a certain darkness into the soul. And this, too, must be accepted with the same open disposition. The darkness will conceal the deeper turn of divine love toward our soul, and in this truth we need to trust much.

~

"If you continue in my word . . ." (Jn 8:31). So evocative a phrase, but what does it require? The first thought may be a need of constant faithfulness to all that Jesus teaches. But maybe that interpretation is not enough, and this phrase asks much more. Perhaps for one thing, it requires that we seek to know the sound of his voice really speaking to us in silence, to experience this, not in a mystical sense, but as a direct personal request to our soul; and then to desire to hear this voice often, with a longing to remain always at his summons. The demand may be for more than simply coming to know his voice; it may also be to have his silence persist in our heart. This implies an effort of inward receptivity, a waiting and a patience to hear from him at a deeper level of recognition in our soul that ordinary language does not penetrate. A training in a different language is therefore necessary. We must develop an attentiveness not focused only on the spoken word, limited to a language we comprehend; rather, we must search for meanings we may not initially hold in our awareness but that come to light later precisely when in prayerful silence we have remained for a time before the gaze of his eyes.

~

An expectation as we begin prayer may open us to new discoveries in reading the Gospel. The words of Jesus, heard many times before, can capture our heart in a completely fresh manner. But why the new insight? Always in these new insights, the presence of his voice accompanies the words we read from the Gospel. A recognition in faith occurs, not just of a new meaning in words that we never considered before, but of his personal presence speaking to us in these words. We can ponder a long time over a passage of the Gospel, and then in a flash the unexpected insight arrives because it is he who speaks to us now in the current hour. This experience is really not comparable to other discoveries we make when some hard work becomes a preparation for a discovery. In the case of the words of Jesus, it is clearly more gratuitous. What has been read in the Gospel with customary familiarity is suddenly radiant with a new significance. But always there is a quality of personal impact in this experience, as though the words are being spoken immediately to our own soul. To continue in his word, then, is, in one sense, to wait for his voice to speak in silence, whether he whispers faintly or pronounces a clear command. It is to listen expectantly for his request, his invitation, by which he enters our soul's privacy and stays there. And so often this occurs through words on a page of the Gospel.

~

Our interpretation of Gospel passages is affected by a quality of loving engagement with the Person of Jesus Christ. A more contemplative response to him in prayer makes us hear him differently. His words are then heard up close and at times provoke a conviction that a deeper, unrecognized meaning lies buried within a simple statement. The awareness of something still untouched, not yet comprehended, resonates in us. There is a link between silent prayer and this experience of reading the Gospels. While reading the words of Jesus, we encounter a sense of mystery similar to our experience in a prayer of inner silence. The awareness of God as hidden and concealed that our soul finds when remaining in silence before God is now transferred to a sense of the imponderable depth in the words of Jesus just read and now resting within our inner spirit. The words have been heard, they have meaning, but there is a further realization that there are meanings still awaiting us, a comprehension that is beyond our ability at this time. Not every passage of the Gospel can evoke this effect. But there are many words of Jesus, especially in Saint John's Gospel, that can give the clear impression of a source in the infinite depths of the divine nature.

One easy example of this truth is his statement to Peter at the washing of the apostles' feet. "What I am doing you do not know now, but afterward you will understand" (Jn 13:7). In the silence of prayer, these words can easily be heard speaking directly to our own heart. Indeed, it is true in a time of trial that we do not know sometimes what he is doing, what purpose is at work. But if we listen in silence, he is speaking to our soul personally at that very hour through these words a promise that later, surely, all will be understood in his loving plan.

~

In our response to the Gospel, a shift must take place from a conviction of the truth residing in the words of Jesus Christ to a direct experience that these same words are making a personal demand in our actual life. It is one thing to assimilate the teaching of the Gospel, even with profound respect and love, taking the instruction of Jesus as a guide for conduct. This is like attending a school and then applying what has been learned in the real circumstances of life. But it is quite another experience to have the Gospel words mysteriously invade our existence with an immediate resonance. The demand of any word of Jesus is far different when in silence we hear the words of Jesus directly addressing our own heart. When he speaks to us his own words, the incomparable new effect is how personal the words have now become. It is like the difference between reading a book and suddenly entering ourselves into the pages as a real character among other characters in that book.

～

The words "I thirst" (Jn 19:28) of Jesus on the Cross cannot be encountered properly without pondering the vinegar offered to his request and his mother Mary's contemplation of this. In that moment, the Virgin Mary remained silent, not moving in the direction of her Son's need. Even as vinegar was poured on hyssop and placed to his lips, still Mary did not move. These words of Jesus near death did not permit her intervention. But her heart drank in the bitter realization. She must have understood the vinegar lifted to his bleeding mouth as a final dereliction. She must have perceived it as a sign of the contempt and indifference for her Son's offering that would remain in some lives for all history. And with her mother's eyes, she must have seen in Jesus' face that he was aware. She surely knew with grace that he had spoken these words as a last testimony of his heart and of his infinite thirst for souls, a heart soon to be pierced in death as a sign for all history. And surely she prayed with her own thirst that souls for all time would recognize the divine longing for souls and not offer him vinegar once again.

～

The response of the Father to the words of Jesus on the Cross is silence. This silence is not in itself a refusal to speak. It is not a sign of rejection. It ought not to be interpreted as an abandonment of Jesus, a withdrawal by his Father into a divine indifference toward the suffering of Jesus. The silence is received by Jesus with love, as it has been throughout his life. In all likelihood, it has always been his practice in prayer to speak few words and to receive from the Father this response of silence. It is no different now on the Cross. The silent voice of the Father in these hours, unlike his voice heard at the Baptism near the Jordan or in Jerusalem close to the events of the Passion, has been the usual manner of the Father's communication to Jesus throughout his life. This silence is the ultimate eloquence, incapable of greater depth. It is the language of an infinite and absolute longing of the Father for Jesus, and Jesus knows it well. He is fluent in the sound of its tones and modulations, in all its secret expressions and idioms. It is a language unlike any other. It does not need a collective chain of words joined together to arrive at clarity and expression. It is eloquent in itself simply by remaining silence.

It is the language of union between the Father and Son, and it is the reason why Jesus speaks so few words on the Cross. There is no need except for our human ears to hear him. The Father already understands perfectly.

~

It is not Scripture alone that sometimes can manifest the truth of God's spoken word and draw our love. In the no-man's-land separating the trenches dug by the Allies and the Germans during the First World War, it was common at night to hear the cries of the dying soldiers stopped by machine gun barrages earlier in the day in the effort to overrun the enemy line. By nighttime the haunted ravings and delirium from the bloody wasteland between the trenches became loud to the soldiers sleepless in their safety. One cry repeated itself over and over —the desperate plea for water—and it continued even in the whispered last breathing of these mortally wounded men. There were no rescues possible for either side, and the nights were long. It is recounted that occasionally those in the trenches broke down and went mad in listening to these cries of thirst. There are places and times in history that bear a strong resemblance to Calvary and echo Jesus' own suffering. In this case, the many lonely deaths in that mud of the no-man's-land, receiving only a silent response in the darkness of a cruel night, recall the last minutes of Jesus' crucifixion and his own cry of thirst.

10

Notes on Contemplative Prayer

"He sought God as if he had never seen him. In the same way, all of those in whom the desire of God is deeply embedded never cease yearning for more. Every delight in God becomes a kindling for a still more ardent desire."

— Saint Gregory of Nyssa

" 'Nought but thyself', replies Saint Thomas to Christ, who asks him what reward he would have. This absence of any return on oneself, this very pure desire of God alone, is the essential condition of contemplation."

— Jacques Maritain

"Our greatest need is to be silent before this great God with the appetite and with the tongue, for the only language He hears is the silent language of love."

— Saint John of the Cross

Certain observations rooted in long traditions regarding contemplative prayer are an aid to understanding the secret hungers the soul undergoes in this prayer. It is easy to become confused or discouraged in the actual interior experience of contemplative prayer. The experiential aspect of the prayer itself is often a contradiction to a soul's expectation of close relations with God. It is beneficial as such to have some knowledge of what to anticipate. The essential teaching repeated over centuries about the nature of contemplative prayer is an aid to discernment and indeed a protection against an unhelpful interpretation of interior darkness that might otherwise be avoided. Contemplative prayer is an exercise of love and an encounter with love, but in both cases it is invariably a self-emptying experience for the soul. The reality of this prayer is truly to place ourselves in the sacred hands of God, who on some days may seem to crush us and on other rarer days to caress us.

The immediacy of a loving knowledge of God received in contemplative prayer leads anyone writing on the subject to speak of an experiential knowledge. "Love itself", writes Saint Gregory the Great, "is a kind of knowing." The knowledge of God in this prayer, in other words, is not primarily given to the mind. It comes through the experience of love, implying more than a mental act. The soul praying does not stand as an observer, so to speak, separated and apart from what is known. Instead, an experience of being drawn into a longing for God is unleashed gently upon the soul, and this experience of a longing for God becomes a manner of knowledge. An awareness of the divine presence comes through the drawing power of the longing felt in prayer. This is not emotional longing, but a deeper undercurrent of desire beneath emotion, obscurely but undeniably carrying the soul in the direction of a real presence beyond self. The sense of distance from God due to his ultimate mystery is for the moment overcome by love. What was known in mystery from afar is perceived now as a sacred personal presence drawing our soul's surrender. Our soul comes to know God by its taste of desire, remaining in blindness, but immediately drawn by the One who is longed for.

～

The grace of infused love given to the soul at the time of silent prayer is a primary factor in contemplative prayer. Infused love produces to some degree a sense of adhesion in our will to a will beyond ourselves. Our soul is being drawn by love toward a beloved, and our own will experiences this as a type of desire and deeper longing within the soul. The grace induces as well a desire within our soul to give of ourselves, and this, too, is felt as a longing within our will. The will feels to some degree its inclination toward Someone other than self. Yet the same grace seems also to draw our soul inward toward its own deepest reality. The adhesion of our will's desire to a longing mysteriously distinct from our own desire seems to take place in a depth within our own soul. This presence of a desire beyond our own desire mingles with our longing to offer ourselves in some complete, entire manner. It is as though God wants nothing more than this longing to offer ourselves completely to him. He then responds to our longing with his desire for our soul.

~

The essential grace behind contemplative prayer is the fusing of an intense longing for God with a deep surrender to him. The graced fusion of these two acts permits contemplative prayer to take place. The difference ordinarily present between these two dispositions fades. They are no longer separate; they merge and become indistinguishable. This coalescence in silence of our soul's yearning for God and our yielding to him makes all deeper prayer possible. The conjoining is the catalyst to an encounter with God within our heart. The combination inflames the soul with an exclusive desire for God. Bringing the two dispositions together seems to invite God in a special way because the soul then has no other desire but for God. The one disposition is never sufficient in itself to open the soul to this mysterious touch of God. These dispositions have to draw together in a sacred fusion. And in their union they provoke a richer longing for God that is incomparable to any ordinary desire. The soul enters at that point into a different hunger for God. The merger of yearning and surrender takes the soul to a much greater depth in its love. God becomes for the moment entirely sought in the soul's craving to surrender all to him. There is nothing for the soul to do but to seek and desire God. The deep longing of the soul to submit and offer all to him becomes in itself an encounter with God and his sacred mystery.

～

A disposition of receptivity so characteristic of contemplative prayer is due to love. But this disposition can never be described accurately as a condition of pure passivity. It is never simply an absence of any interior act. It is not to remain inert or numb or dull. It involves at times a choice of waiting, of listening, of loving attentiveness to God, and all this with a kind of charged undercurrent of desire within the soul. It demands as well a contemplative passion for silence in prayer and an implicit realization that silence has unsuspected depths within our soul. This quality of receptivity within the quiet of prayer may require a certain training for a time,

a practice of mental austerity and a refusal to turn
to easier satisfactions for the mind. Thoughts do
not calm down unless some deeper attentiveness
replaces an interest in them and leaves them alone.
A spirit of accessibility to God is the primary need
for this deeper attentiveness. This interior disposition is equivalent to letting God decide everything,
which includes what he will do, not only with the
current hour, but with our whole life, which belongs entirely to him. Receptivity as a disposition
in prayer is inseparable in this sense from a recognition of belonging to God in the entirety of our
lives.

～

On some occasions, receptivity in contemplative
prayer will mean undergoing a painful hunger while
refusing to assuage it. The soul in prayer must take
care not to be released from it. This impoverishment takes place inasmuch as everything in us belongs only all to God. It deepens to the degree
that we make no effort to overcome this realization of our poverty. In that sense, we must be receptive, open, accessible to becoming more poor.
The poverty is the dispossession caused by seeking
and not finding, desiring and not attaining, longing and not taking hold in any possession. Being
consumed with a desire that goes unsatisfied when
nothing else can be desired is a sure path to inte-

rior poverty. This poverty will mean at times being trapped in dissatisfaction, caught in a corner of the soul and unable to extricate ourselves, blocked by an impasse without any sign of what to seek as a next step. By our receptivity to God in prayer, however, even in such poverty, our soul will never be at a loss. In one sense, we may seem to suffer a perpetual anticipation of a fulfillment that never arrives. On the other hand, a promise is already being confirmed. Our soul needs only to wait for God to show his divine longing in a deeper, unfelt region of the soul, so that it may enter that longing where God alone is everything. The receptivity of our soul is the door into this intense longing for God.

∼

Waiting, expectation, anticipation—the capacity to keep vigil in prayer and await the One who is desired is a crucial contemplative need. To wait, however, is also to remain in a state of dissatisfaction. But this discontent must be endured without focusing attention on how long the wait seems to be extended. Our attention must turn its gaze only to the One who is desired, ready to remain in that state of waiting for a prolonged time, if necessary, knowing only that often he has already arrived even when there is nothing to show it. This knowledge is enough for us to remain attentive in longing and keep us from leaving prayer. "It is yearning", Saint Augustine reminds us, "that makes the heart deep."

~

The quality of "passivity" peculiar to contemplative prayer does require a careful interpretation. The mistake in some explanations can be to view this passivity solely as an indifference toward mental operations, a practice of non-engagement with thoughts in order to "let things happen" without any effort to control. Those who counsel this false type of passivity urge no resistance to the flow of random thoughts and images passing through our mind, which will come and go inasmuch as they are not pursued or treated with interest. The idea is that a tranquility of mind is thus achieved by this absence of struggle. After a time, no great effort is needed to recover the same state of a disinterested mind in prayer. It demands only following the same procedure of non-engagement with particular thoughts. In contrast, the true passivity of contemplative life is really not passive in the exact sense of the word, and it is not directed to the presence of thoughts in prayer. This genuine passivity is an active inward disposition of receptive attentiveness and love toward God. In true contemplative life, an expectant yearning is present in the soul; real desire animates the inner spirit and makes it receptive in its longing for God. The passive dimension is in the waiting, in the patient expectation, that accompanies a receptive disposition. Desire in the soul for God remains poised and taut, as it were, inasmuch as the soul hungers without satiation. At the same time, this form of contemplative passivity renounces any effort of direct pursuit, as we might exercise in a chase after an immediate target in front of us. The passivity consists, rather, in remaining still, waiting, anticipating the unseen presence that will draw our soul and incline us to want nothing but to give ourselves to him. This passivity is to be actively receptive to the desire to love in return for love.

~

At the same time, there is ordinarily no deeper contemplative stillness in prayer unless our mind becomes empty of particular thoughts. Only when our mind has nothing to occupy it and is empty of thought does silence permeate a deeper realm of our soul. Until then, there is often at best a struggle for calm and quiet in our soul. This other deeper dimension of receptive silence brings with it a quality of attention, but without a focus on any particular thought. It offers a different taste from simply a cultivated concentration. It is a silence that draws a definite attraction from our soul, namely, a surrender of all of ourself to God. Nothing holds our attention in that silence but a longing to give our entire self to him. This desire to surrender everything of ourselves to God is precisely what makes this deeper silence an experience of self-emptying. It requires no effort for our soul, for we want nothing else in that hour but to be empty of self and to surrender ourselves to God. An unconcern for self permeates our soul at such times, just as the silence seems to surround and support this same loss of thought for self. No thought for self occupies the mind in this state of empty attention. Instead, all attentiveness is turned to God, without a particular thought. Our soul has in a sense become lost in a blind desire leaning in love toward the infinite mystery of God.

～

On the other hand, if our mind does turn to thoughts in that time, even thoughts about God, the desire for God seems quickly to disappear. It is a strange thing that this should happen, but perhaps it has an explanation. The leaning of the mind by some deliberate, willed effort toward a particular thought or reflection takes us from the true grace of the prayer at that moment. Every deeper contemplative encounter with God depends on a harmony between the two inner states of an interior stillness within self and an emptiness of self. These two dispositions must combine. Their union and joining ignites the soul with the flaming desire to surrender everything of self to God. But they also imply that there is no deliberate effort to engage ourselves in reflective thought at that time.

∼

When contemplative insights occur and are received in silent prayer, they are usually not immediate lights that can be translated so quickly into useful thoughts. These insights may not bring clear thoughts at all but only a mere beginning or suggestion of a reflection. Certainly no extended commentary accompanies them that we might carry away from an hour of prayer. These moments of recognition, in their usual pattern, simply convey a certitude of a truth known in faith. Or, more strongly, they convince us that someone infinitely holy is the real presence we are meeting blindly in prayer, without sight, often without any feeling. In all deeper prayer, we come to know God with an undeniable certainty. This awareness of God is a recognition beyond thought, without an explanation of any sort. Often it involves a silencing and simplifying of thought to a single, unimpeded awareness that he is present, and that is enough. We are joined to a loving gaze, united in a manner beyond our understanding to someone else's thought and gaze. The recognition of this becomes, then, an immediate cause for gratitude and wonder. If there are insights gained from the experience, they seem to flow beyond the time of prayer itself and provide light when we return to some effort of reflection.

~

Impatience for vision is contrary to the contemplative demand for waiting in a state of blindness. We have to avoid forcing to the forefront of our thought some clear notion that will provide contentment to our mind in prayer. The desire to see is understandable and will not disappear, for it is intrinsic to the desire of contemplative love and to our mind's natural desire. At the same time, this longing to see will never be satisfied. Our soul must accept the hunger to see as a permanent condition of dissatisfaction in our relations with God. Satiation in any type of spiritual "seeing" would imply an arrival that can never take place in this life. If there is any semblance of sight and comprehension intermittently given in our prayer, it is meant primarily to arouse in us a greater impatience of love. It is not strictly for the sake of an insight alone.

~

Consciousness can certainly be burned darkly in contemplative prayer, in the smoldering wait for a fruitful thought, with nothing to capture interest or invite reflection. The emptiness of thought at such times is not chosen; it is only suffered. As long as we are attentive and turned in longing toward God, however, this absence of thought should not trouble our soul. It diminishes as a concern as long as we maintain the conviction of resting in another's gaze. "I sat down in the shadow of the one I have longed for." This phrase, a slight alteration of words from the Song of Songs (Song 2:3), captures well the essential need. The limits of our mind in prayer are not shared by our heart's yearning. There is no limitation to our longing for God, and this loving attention we can direct toward God is a primary reality of this prayer. There is no need to seek relief when all is well. We are not so alone as we sometimes may think, nor are we unassisted. Over time the inadequacy of every partial thought about God will simply assert itself more implacably, and that is fine. Rather than seeking glimpses of truth, it is better to accept that an effort to think about God can simply be a distraction. What we want is God himself, not an idea to tantalize our interest. When we remain in a blind yearning for God, we may more easily awaken, to our own surprise, ". . . like the sleeper who, arising from a

lengthy sleep, opens his eyes to the sight of an unexpected light" (Saint John of the Cross).

∽

No soul that plunges more fully into contemplative
relations with God can escape the sense of blun-
dering on occasion into a blind alley from which
there is no easy way out. The unfamiliar suddenly
surrounds our soul on all sides, and there is no obvious direction to take. This uncertainty may be
part of any serious search for God and his will.
But it is also inseparable from an experience of dying to self, which takes place sometimes by walk-
ing ahead without clear assurances, without any
promise that a clear path is about to open up and
become known. It is difficult to imagine that absolute self-confidence is compatible with this uncertainty. Sometimes only tentative steps in life can
be taken, even if we trust that we are being led,
while at other times we may seem stuck and not
moving and can only cling to God. These experiences can hardly be compared to the easy strides
of a runner with the finish line in sight. And yet
through it all, God somehow does keep us from
irreversible mistakes, a realization often made only
in hindsight, but one to provoke much gratitude.

∽

An intense desire for prayer is often matched by a painful frustration when the opportunity for prayer arrives. The desire we bring to prayer shifts somehow in the course of silent prayer to an intense dissatisfaction of soul. This experience is something out of our control; indeed, it contradicts the expectation we carry into prayer. We bring a flame of longing into a chapel and depart with ashes in our hand and spent fire. We wish to gaze toward the distant beauty of a vast horizon, and we find ourselves enclosed behind walls of dry silence and shadow. We hope for a sacred encounter in the cloister of the heart and, instead, get waylaid in a place of restless loneliness. The companion we seek is late, then does not arrive, and finally we leave. Yet the yearning burns on. The fire is not exhausted; the flame simmers beneath the cover of ashes. The longing that is covered over in dissatisfaction takes us to a greater desire for offering and renunciation. But it is an offering of our soul in emptiness and poor nakedness—and perhaps more pleasing to God for that reason.

~

The rapid shift of experience from one day to the next in prayer is certainly disconcerting to some souls. It is not uncommon, after the gaze of love cast upon our soul, to become quickly a stranger again, a foreigner to intimacy with God. The experience is shocking because love in prayer seems always to promise permanence. It is impossible to consider otherwise. The longing of the soul for God is embraced in a manner that extends beyond any limit of the current encounter in prayer. And yet the hour does pass, followed soon by a frozen hour of distance and detachment, strangely cold and intimidating in the impression it can give of its finality and the fixed disregard of One whose eyes after much love seem now to be averted, turned away in disappointed recoil. These shifting alterations of experience in prayer, without any predictable measure, require at the very least that hope accompany the poverty of the more difficult hours in prayer. For in the difficult hours it can seem there will be no more encounter with God. Deeper prayer is not for the fainthearted but for those who can persevere in hope.

∼

The insecurity of love when love is unfelt is actually a fortunate experience in contemplative prayer if taken in the right way. It is meant to foster greater generosity in our soul. And this response of greater self-giving is above all true in the life of contemplative prayer. Our desire to offer ourselves to God can be most generous and can release its fullest effect on our soul precisely when there is no feeling of a return for the act of love we have just made in the silence of the heart. The deepening trust that there is an objective reality to this act of offering regardless of the personal experience of it takes greater hold over time. The act of offering need not be measured by any subjective consideration. It is understood after a while to pierce the heart of God even when it leaves our own heart still unsatisfied.

~

We must simply accept at times the sense of unpleasant restraint that comes unexpectedly into the life of prayer and sometime lasts for long periods, a testing that seems to fasten the soul down and confine it to restricted boundaries as though tethered by a rope, without the prospect of ranging beyond the already familiar thought and desire. It reminds us that we do not control and determine the experience of prayer. We can seek to avoid mistakes and steer clear of impediments, but we cannot open doors freely on our own to a deeper experience of God. Prayer is one of the great adventures, but like many adventures, it can find itself unsure where it has now arrived or how long the current halt in the journey will last. All ultimately depends on how

God wants our soul to be drawn into a complete offering to him.

⌒

The occasional anxiety that can afflict interior prayer may seem to have no reason or explanation. But perhaps it is linked to a purification that occurs when we are renouncing ourselves for love of God. Abnegation of self, when it goes beyond mere ascetical sacrifice and cuts deeply into the soul, can bring a strange insecurity to silent prayer, as though we were losing our foothold in the uphill journey to God and unable to hold our step in place. It is possible to feel lost then in the silence of prayer, directionless, without familiar markings to map our way. But perhaps this is the symptom of something more significant than just a temporary inner confusion. Our soul may be discovering its truth before God, which means it is being stripped down to its nothingness, emptied in itself as an entity apart from God's love. If that is so, we must ignore these insecurities and simply return to the essential offering of ourselves to God. If God prefers everything for the moment to remain dark and unrecognizable and wants only our blind surrender, there is no reason to be anxious. It is always enough in silent prayer, no matter what is experienced, to offer ourselves to his choice alone. And that divine choice includes the inexplicable and dark experiences that can accompany silent prayer. In the end, every act of deeper self-offering to God places us firmly again before the gaze of God.

~

There is an answer that all contemplative souls must discover for themselves. The internal quality in contemplative prayer of *wanting* God, of our thirst and need for him, must be joined to an act of gratitude when our desire goes unslaked. At first it seems impossible for gratitude to be expressed when no satisfaction in prayer occurs. But this gratitude for *every* experience in prayer is important. Without it, the frustration of our desire may turn to a kind of subdued resentment, which can only diminish love. But gratitude, even as a consciously willed act, implies a recognition that all is not seen, that much in this life of prayerfully seeking God still awaits discovery and an ultimate unveiling. Gratitude while undergoing deprivation opens us to the deeper realization that God is unfathomable in his sacred ways of love. The mystery of God is not only in the divine nature itself but in the gestures of engagement by which he takes our soul to his heart. He is a hidden God, but he is always near in his hiddenness. When we express gratitude to him in a blind or uncomprehending condition, accepting calmly the fact that we do not see, yet certain of the loving presence that is always near, we reach already by that act into the heart of God.

∼

In all this varying experience, contemplative souls know by an instinct of love that a secret exchange with God is taking place in their lives. But they know also that this private exchange with God leaves no permanent satisfactions. The soul has to return each day to the unpredictable seeking in prayer, not knowing what awaits it. They know from long experience how foolish it is to anticipate what will happen in prayer. Disappointment too often follows when the soul fixes its desire on any particular experience of God. God drawing a soul to himself is always a secret for that soul alone, and usually even the soul itself does not understand. The contemplative can be tempted to think there is nothing so personal in any divine gesture to it. In that sense, prayer can be deceptive. It can be like reaching out to the hands of a loved one and clasping only air in an empty grip —when in fact the hands one sought are gently wrapped around one's shoulders. And one cannot say which experience—the certitude of closeness or the agony of absence—is the more direct and personal encounter with God. Prayer has no real scale of measurement, no criterion to distinguish the better from the worse. The contrasting encounters with God extend down the nights and days of a life. Who can say which experiences in prayer are more profitable for a soul? It may be that the painful experiences of prayer bring much more grace to a soul precisely because they, too, are full of the personal presence of God, and a soul is more a humble beggar in them.

11

Bedrock Faith and Contemplation

"The higher he ascends the less he understands, because the cloud is dark which lit up the night; whoever knows this remains always in unknowing and transcending all knowledge."

—Saint John of the Cross

"The Gospel written in men's hearts goes far beyond the written text, despite the fact that what is written is itself, in a sense, inexhaustible. The Fathers were well aware of this."

—Yves Congar, O.P.

"Faith does not quench desire, but inflames it."

—Saint Thomas Aquinas

The contemplative must lean on pure faith, as Saint John of the Cross affirms insistently. By this teaching, he maintains that our hunger for God in prayer depends in an absolute sense on a belief in his immediate presence to our soul despite what can seem at times the stark emptiness of the dark hour. In this teaching, faith is essential to the con-templative life, just as breathing is to the human person. The certitude upon which the deeper life of contemplative prayer rests can only be firmly grounded in the unquestion-ing dispositions of a soul's deeper faith. Faith establishes the certitude of the divine presence, without which prayer might be thought simply a lonely cry released into the vast reaches of an empty night. By faith our soul knows that prayer draws a mysterious response from God, even when it seems to be an answer of silence. The silence conceals God's longing for our soul—a truth known often only by faith. It is a faith always rooted in the clear teaching of the Catholic doctrinal tradition, without which no contempla-tive life can survive.

The truth of God is an inexhaustible mystery and therefore always an incitement and goad to our intelligence. Even with an intensity of faith, we confront the incomprehensibility of God. There is no eventual arrival in prayer at a comfortable knowledge of God. He is infinite love and beyond our human understanding. Contrary to what may be our expectation, greater faith does not grant a more expansive knowledge of God. What it does more often is reduce our knowledge of him to a blind certitude of his living presence. We realize in deeper prayer how real he is and, likewise, how unknown he still is. This inability to overcome barriers of blindness in our knowledge of God is the normal condition of contemplative prayer after a certain point. Over time, we learn more about the limits of knowledge, while at the same time recognizing that there is no limit to love. A loving encounter with God can remain our great desire in prayer even in blindness and incomprehension. And God, indeed, does make the reality of his presence known at times, though not perhaps to our satisfaction. For his presence is not a reality that the soul, even with great love, can embrace as a possession. Always God slips back into hiding, so that our love, too, may be inexhaustible.

~

The revealed truths of Christianity not only lay bare the face of God. They convey as well his ultimate concealment in mystery and transcendence. They confront us with his hiding and his elusiveness, even while bringing the gift of his presence and companionship. The paradox of our relations with God is contained in this dual aspect of revealed truth. Revelation does not present us merely with the truth of who God is, thereby releasing us from wrestling with an ultimate mystery. The exposure of the truth of God to us in Jesus Christ has intensified the mystery of God. By allowing us to see his divine love in the face, the words, the acts of a particular historical man, Jesus of Nazareth, God has only deepened our encounter with his transcendent mystery as infinite love. The experience of this paradox is available primarily in two encounters: by showing us his infinite love in the crucifixion of Jesus and, then, once again in the concealed sacramental presence of Jesus Christ in the Eucharist. Who can look upon the hours of that dark day at Calvary and not find God more inexhaustible and unfathomable in his reality? And who can gaze on the appearance of Bread in the Eucharist and not find him beyond words? We confront more mystery in God at Calvary and in a chapel of Eucharistic exposition than in any possible speculation on God's vast and immeasurable grandeur. Drawing closer to God will always demand the search for him in the swirling dust of Jerusalem on that last Friday of his short life and on our knees before a tabernacle or monstrance. The presence of our God in the disfigured, bleeding man undergoing a horrible Roman crucifixion, his identity as God, is an ultimate mystery that continues to conceal God from us. The Eucharist, too, fragile and concealed, presents him blindly before our eyes. His silence at Golgotha, his marred face, his brief words, submerge us in a dizzying, imperceptible place of direct encounter with God. Direct, also, is his gaze on us from a tabernacle or monstrance. His hour of darkness at Calvary exposes to our love the face of

God. Can we ever love him enough while looking upon this mystery of his crucified divine presence in the Eucharist?

~

Much has been written about his Passion, and yet there are no words to explain it. Our faith undergoes a radical deepening with the awareness that we cannot understand such love. Our encounter with the hill of Calvary confronts a realm of cloud and shadow we can never lift by our own effort. In our searching for God at Calvary, there is always a failure to understand fully. Only a recognition by love is possible. And if we persevere in an awareness that our God is speaking personally to us in this event of Calvary, he will be loved differently because his love will be perceived differently. For the sake of that more intense recognition of love, we ought to pray that our faith not remain simply peaceful. We should allow our faith to know the disturbing upheaval and convulsion of being shaken at the foot of that Roman Cross in Jerusalem.

~

The sacred mystery of God does not submit simply to the mute words on a printed page. His mystery is never by human language alone laid open and unveiled. Neither the propositions of Catholic doctrine nor the revealed texts of Scripture pierce entirely his divine secrecy. In a certain sense, God evades every effort of human words to disclose his ultimate reality, and this is true even of biblical language. At the same time, precise, accurate words have special importance in doctrinal statements about God. And the words of the Bible are in truth God's spoken word to us. Yet in both cases the truth enunciated in human language is directed to the infinite mystery in God himself. Knowing God in truth therefore demands more than an encounter with a written word. This knowledge must take place for each soul in a silence beneath words. Our encounter with God cannot be simply a knowledge received from a sacred book or a catechism. Contact with words in a book, even when that book is the Bible, is never the same as meeting God in a personal manner, especially in praying before the Blessed Sacrament. It is only in silence, when words have exhausted their value and serve no more purpose, that a deeper awareness of God's secret presence is sometimes given to our soul, and then the words themselves we encounter in Scripture are transformed. This kind of knowledge is nonetheless irreducible to words. Thought alone cannot arrive at this discovery or comprehend it. Words are often no help at all, and no expression in words can afterward describe the sense of his presence speaking. Language at such times simply subsides like the ocean waves dropping away on the seashore, replaced by the greater eloquence of silence.

∼

Christianity is the religion of divine revelation. God has spoken to us in his Son, the divine Word. Divine revelation is to look at Jesus and hear his words, not as though God transmitted a message through him, making use of a singular emissary. In truth, Jesus is the Almighty One pronouncing his own words and speech to our ears. Divine revelation is nothing less than Jesus Christ himself. The simplicity of our own task in faith is concentrated in this truth. But a second simplicity is necessary in our faith. The revelation of God in the man Jesus of Nazareth and the transcendent mystery of God are not separate truths. They are not truths somehow in tension. They join together as the ultimate truth of God. Our faith exposes to us the fact that God in his infinite goodness and love is seen and heard in the person of Jesus Christ. But this means that the divinity of Jesus remains also a mystery beyond our grasp. Faith reveals the truth of God speaking and acting in Jesus. But our faith realizes as well that he is concealed from our complete comprehension. The hidden mystery of the Trinity always accompanies the presence of Jesus

Christ. He is heard and seen, and yet always the Father and the Holy Spirit hover in mystery and oneness with him. And this truth plunges us always in our prayer into a deeper wonder and an incapacity of understanding.

∼

If our relations with God become cerebral, too dominated by an intellectual approach, as can happen when theological reading occupies much interest, a certain antipathy for searching more deeply into the sacred mystery of God can occur. When the mind monopolizes what should be a personal quest for God, ideas about God may serve largely to detach us from him. They place God at a distant remove, like an impressive mountain gazed at from far away. An aspect or attribute of God can become a question that must be investigated, analyzed, reduced to some semblance of clarity. Indeed, the mystery of God can be treated simply as an intellectual conundrum. But God resists such efforts when they include no need for personal encounter. The result is that thoughts about God, when they lack a yearning for real contact with God, will likely become impersonal ideas. His actual truth will be inaccessible to our awareness. The only answer to this detour in relations with

God is the return to a tabernacle and falling again upon our knees.

~

The devil is a great liar, as Jesus warns, which means that his primary target is our intelligence. His effort is to work his whisper within the quiet of the mind without detection, unknown until the damage is done. One observation would seem undeniable. With fixed, persevering intent, he seeks to undermine a soul's attraction for the attainability of truth. He wants to replace a hunger for spiritual truth with an acquiescence to permanent uncertainties and confusion. The truth of Christianity is of course the primary concentration of his attack. A soul's conviction in faith is the ultimate prize he pursues. In subtle whispers, he poses objections, raises doubts, insinuates the likelihood of false, unreasonable assumptions. He exaggerates and distorts what is sometimes called the irrationality of religious belief. He has a special love for useless questioning that has no end point, for reflections that veer off into idiosyncratic byways and tangents. His deceptions are often couched in common sense logic. Other times he provokes hyperrational brooding and strained complications of argument. He loves to bait a soul with a remembrance of its native intelligence and a need to think independently, without reliance on any authority for truth other than a personal determination of truth. What can be surprising is that no contemplative soul is immune from these efforts of the evil one. It is a form of his disrespect for God that he does not consider the contemplative beyond the pale of his possible victory.

~

We walk down a blind alley to a blocked endpoint whenever our mind turns God into a problem we are unable to solve. Without realizing what is happening, our intelligence drains itself in this effort. It is like looking at God through a rusted screen of problematic questions. The mind will find no satisfying answers. Worse, it formulates answers that forget the transcendent mystery of God. A manageable abstraction is never equivalent to the truth of the transcendent reality of God. Ironically, the neglect of God's ultimate transcendence is in turn a way of forsaking his personal nearness to our human soul. Without a more fundamental search for God in his personal reality, precisely as one who is beyond the grasp of our intelligence, the mystery of God simply enervates human intelligence. We may find for a time some contentment in our exercise of thought, but in thinking about God these are the satisfactions ordinarily of cleverness. The great danger is that God as a real person will be lost as an engagement for our thought. Our desire for knowing him will dry up and fade. We will become indifferent to him and to prayer itself.

~

When Saint John of the Cross used the word "inaccessible" in reference to God, he was describing the concealment of God to our soul, which is very different from speaking of him simply as a "problem" to understand. He was stressing the impossibility of our soul crossing certain inflexible barriers in our comprehension of God's ultimate mystery. He was acknowledging the impenetrable mystery in God that no soul can overcome in this life. The same saint, however, insisted that love is inflamed by desire for an ultimate possession of God. Love of its nature longs for this possession, even as it is impossible in this life. This difference between our comprehension of God and our encounter with him by love is an important distinction in prayer. What we often cannot do in prayer is gain new insight and knowledge beyond a certain boundary. What we can do in prayer, by contrast, is by love to allow him to possess us. This will require on our part that we freely surrender to an emptying of ourselves. It is through our own accessibility to God's action in prayer that his concealment becomes, not a strain in our relations with God, but an incitement to a greater self-giving of our soul.

~

This word "inaccessible", as used by Saint John of the Cross, has to be understood on two levels. There is a twofold tension facing our soul in its pursuit of God. The word would be misinterpreted if taken to mean a strict, inviolable boundary between God and our soul that cannot be crossed. This would suggest an insurmountable distance, almost a severance from contact with the heart of God. The thought conveys an image of God detached and empty of desire for his own child. Such a description clearly implies an erroneous notion. Rather, the inaccessibility of God refers only to the barrier of incomprehension that our human mind confronts in facing the infinite nature of God. In contrast with our mind's limitation, we can know something quite differently by love. The accessibility of God's presence to our soul is by love. We are capable of real personal encounters with him in prayer. We can know him as one who enters a door in the soul once we open it for him. We can be aware, even in the extended stretches of silence that resemble a prolonged inaccessibility, that he listens to our longing and to our words of love

and, indeed, to every silent word we speak from
our heart to his heart.

~

For the sake of a contemplative life of deeper faith,
a proper understanding is necessary of an apophatic
"unknowing" in the soul's relations with God.
This understanding casts light as well on the use
of the term inaccessibility in Saint John of the
Cross' language about God. A rationalistic conception of the apophatic "state of unknowing" raises
objections that misunderstand it. The rationalist
interpretation identifies this state of unknowing as
a form of agnostic uncertainty about God. The
apophatic way can then sound like a descent into a
tunnel of dim shadows. The state of unknowing the
soul experiences can be falsely depicted as a deliberate closing down of the mind, a plunge into cultivated inner emptiness. The apophatic experience
in prayer would appear in this view to be a voluntary immersion in an unhealthy darkness. But this
is misleading and inaccurate. The so-called condition of "unknowing" is not deliberately sought.
The description of a state of unknowing, indeed
the precise choice of such words, is an effort to
expose an experiential truth in prayer. The soul in
contemplative prayer undergoes a silencing of the

mind due to the overwhelming excess of reality in every deeper encounter with God. This experience cannot be identified as mystical experience in it-self. Yet it is essential as an experience to contemplative prayer. The mind finds itself tied down and bound, fastened and unable to move—not crippled or desperate for assistance—but as though incapacitated and unable to leap toward God with any deeper awareness and recognition. Perhaps there is a helpful explanation for this phenomenon. Sometimes in love one must close one's eyes to see better the beauty of the beloved. The apophatic experience in prayer reflects such a requirement in love —one's perception must be conquered by love, indeed, made blind by love. The loss of sight may not be appealing to a rationalist point of view. But with love this can be understood and accepted. There is no need for explanation when love is burning behind the experience.

∽

A misery like unrelieved hunger can gnaw at the soul making advances in a contemplative love for God. When steady and unremitting, the experience cannot be reduced to a mere frustration with the infrequency of any felt consolation in prayer, which may not matter so much after a while. Nor can it be simply categorized under a label of purification. Another insight into the reality of our encounter with God is possible. No soul that crosses the threshold of contemplative relations with God escapes a confrontation with the infinity of God. His divine nature, his love, is immeasurable and overwhelming precisely in prayer—a vast ocean enveloping a grain of sand. At best we brush up against this love without a perception, in a blind manner, without knowing at what we are gazing, unable to gain any clear sense of how close God really is when all is dark and we do not see or comprehend. We can desire with intensity a closer sight, but the distance is too great. In this life a glimpse of infinite love never occurs. Prayer of this nature, then, has really no adequate description. We can turn in the direction of infinite love, but we cannot touch God as infinite, and surely we cannot see him in his infinite nature. All that can be said of his infinite love is spoken from incomprehension. And yet what is known is the longing in us to draw closer to this most desired love. It is enough to know that God himself in his own infinite manner of touch is reaching out to our soul's surrender to him.

～

To remain steadfast in faith while our act of believing is blind and befogged in shadows has no resemblance at all to a deliberate choice to place matters of faith in doubt. What can seem to be a diminishment of certitude in faith is the decline of sight that affects the eyes of faith in a time of spiritual darkness. This is the difficulty of faith when it is undergoing purification, a trial and a stage of growth in faith's advancement. There is another form of incertitude, however, that comes from deliberately suspending one's belief, suppressing a former trust and replacing it with a spirit of indecisiveness and vague hesitancy about faith. Then an opposite orientation is at work. A soul will be tempted to lean in the direction of superficial clarity and easier convictions. At the very least this will mean halting faith's advancement as a virtue. But it may also be the beginning of a turning away from faith. The trial of darkness experienced in faith either takes a soul to deeper waters, or, when not understood, it undermines and depletes faith.

∽

Every soul stretching in deeper faith undergoes this dimming of sight. The diminished clarity in exchange for a deeper certitude in faith is not a contradiction. For Saint John of the Cross, it is a clear sign of advancement in faith. The more intense certitude coupled with a loss of clarity is not optional. It does not occur only for those who would practice such a spirituality. But because it is a confusing experience, especially at first, no one enters upon this darker experience of faith without some strain and suffering and often with a need for some guidance. It is not always possible to find such aid, and not everyone is inclined to turn to Saint John of the Cross for explanation and direction. Somehow, though, God takes care of souls when they remain poor and begging, and most especially perhaps if they are alone. In this case, alone and in need, it is likely that the soul attracts God's compassion and his watchful hand. He does not allow it to stumble in blindness as long as the soul remains humble.

~

Qualitative leaps in religious perception inevitably occur as we continue a contemplative life of faith. But this does not mean seeing more of God or enjoying more tangible relations with him. On the contrary, it is more likely to bring the onset of greater blindness. After a certain point in the experience of deepening faith, interior darkness is simply the more common and steady condition of soul. The shadows of night begin to unfurl with consistent regularity, obscuring the brilliance of spiritual truths. These truths are not covered over as though nothing is seen at all. It is more like a shift to the nighttime shine of moonlight after the day's sun has disappeared. At that point, a trust in God has to replace clarity. Deep, unquestioning certitude of his real presence in mystery is now the supreme need. One blind step at a time must suffice, for the longer view is not possible.

12

Contemplative Hurdles and Stumbling Blocks

"The true vision and the true knowledge of what we seek consists precisely in not seeing, in an awareness that our goal transcends all knowledge and is everywhere cut off from us by the darkness of incomprehensibility."

—Saint Gregory of Nyssa

"When he is thought to be absent, he is seen— when he is present he is not seen."

—Saint Augustine

"We must distinguish clearly between the feeling of possession and the actual possession of God. There are countless souls who possess God who derive no pleasure from that fact."

—Augustin Guillerand

Trials are bound to accompany every spiritual life. But the peculiar form of testing that is likely to afflict contemplative life is generally some variation of a trial of faith.

This does not mean to face doubt about Christian faith but, rather, to undergo some confusion or turmoil in the interior experience of faith. The so-called dark night of faith is not a diminishment of faith but an experience of faith's obscurity as a spiritual life deepens in an intense desire for God. Another obstacle joined to the difficulty of knowing God in a deeper contemplative faith seems to be a common hazard. The desire for a personal experience of God is a great longing precisely for a soul serious about prayer. This same desire, however, can open a path to erroneous interpretations. The nature of interior religious experience has an inherent ambiguity. It requires a sober quality of reflection. If it is not subject to careful scrutiny and examination, there is an easy avenue to mistaken notions of God's immediate accessibility to our experience that violate the essential truth of his divine transcendence.

If we persevere in a steady practice of silent prayer, there are surely inner testings and trials. It is possible, for instance, that for periods of time we will seem to experience nothing of God but our distance from him and a numbing disengagement from his presence. The thought can arise that our passion for God has been lost permanently, swept away by some chill wind on a day we can no longer remember. As the days stretch one into another, we can easily think that our longing for God will never return. There can be a fear that from now on we will find in prayer only the bare solitude of an uncommunicative silence and that nothing will change. But we should not yield to such fears. There is always a poverty hiding in the hours of silent prayer and waiting for us. It seems to catch up with every soul that is resolute in seeking God in silent prayer.

~

We must come to know this poverty in prayer just as we may have learned to know the poor outside prayer. The misery of the really poor can be frightening at first encounter. But it does not remain so. Later the same poverty can draw our soul and become intensely attractive because we recognize a unique human face of misery in that suffering. The same must happen in prayer in a certain sense. An attraction for the greater gift of ourselves that is possible only in a deeper taste of our interior poverty in prayer can begin to draw us. We do not have to make a great effort to come to this realization. If we are faithful to prayer, the poverty of a shadowed interior life will come to us whether we want it or not. We should re-sist, however, the lack of courage that would halt along the darkened path. It is God who is always near, even in darkness and interior poverty, leading our soul one faltering step at a time toward him-self. This path may be enclosed in a dark silence that we had not anticipated and therefore will find initially intimidating. But that same obscure silence is never without a voice of longing for our soul that can be heard in secrecy when we confidently accept in faith that this silence hides Our Lord's loving presence within us.

~

Sometimes those who seem most peaceful and secure in religious belief lack a deeper engagement with its truth. There is an absence of fire in the heart for the real mystery of God. The result is a kind of impermeability of soul to the actual difficulty of seeking God in his personal presence during a lifetime. Certainly the possession of correct belief and fidelity to it are indispensable for religious living. They are ordinarily a source of peace and inner certitude in the soul. But it is the passionate engagement with God that not only makes the life of faith costly but allows it to deepen. We may be perplexed to hear that faith should bring difficulty to our soul. The opposite, it seems, should be the case. But that may not in fact be true. Despite what is often assumed, the entry into faith's greater intensity comes for many souls after a threshold of struggle has been crossed. The struggle is not with a diminishment of faith but, rather, with the effects of a deeper passion for God. This struggle is not sought; in no way is it a deliberate cultivation of doubt or questioning. The difficulty with becoming more passionate for God is that interior darkness often becomes a kind of enclosure within which that passion must live. The darkness seems to cloud the gaze of faith, when in fact it invites a more intense faith. The only option then is to believe more passionately and to pray with more passion, which usually means an unfelt passion of the soul. With this choice comes an increasing certainty that God is indeed quite near. Even blind and overcome by the night, the soul learns a different sense of the presence of God, which it cannot see or feel but knows nonetheless. It senses this presence only in faith, a presence outside feeling but returning, continually near.

$\sim$

For some people, deeper faith will indeed cause at times an essential insecurity in the soul—a fact quite contrary to the assumption that people believe because they lack the courage to live without the comfort of religious promises. But what is this insecurity which faith seems to provoke, especially in contemplative souls? It seems to have a source precisely in an effect of deeper faith. The person who believes more intensely desires a real encounter with God, and yet God does not satisfy this longing so readily. It takes perhaps many

years of purification and a deepening response to
God before a soul seeking God gains an abiding,
irreversible certitude of the Lord's near presence in
life. Before that time, faith may be accompanied by
many extended interludes of darkness and shadow.
The insecurity of soul occurs because the person
firmly believes and yet receives little sense of tangible assurance from faith. It is often the mark of
a greater, more intense faith to endure faith's obscurity and yet persevere in an unyielding commitment to the invisible truths known in faith. There
is a quiet heroism of the spiritual realm in the lives
of such souls.

~

There is an enormous difference between denying
God and the spiritual trial of suffering the absence
of God. A trial of this sort is never an early experience in a spiritual life. If this trial occurs, it is only
after a soul has spent many silent hours with God
in prayer. And no doubt it has faced many trials already in which the pattern of God's disappearance
and eventual return has been displayed. Ordinarily,
then, a soul undergoing a new taste of confusion
and darkness never releases a firm grip on faith.
Yet for someone in the midst of this suffering, it
can seem difficult to distinguish the experience of
internal darkness from a collapse of the certainty of
faith. Profound faith can be joined to what seems a

helpless descent into a condition of incertitude and even doubt. The shadows enclosing a soul can give the impression that it is slipping close to a precipice over which, unless a rescue takes place, it will soon fall. But this fear is unfounded. And it is primarily without justification because God invariably protects a soul that cleaves to him. He holds carefully by the hand the soul that has learned never to let go. God may allow that soul to endure blindness for a time. But this is never a perpetual state, and soon enough some sign of his near presence jolts the soul anew with recognition and gratitude.

∿

It is one thing to assent in faith comforted by the clear light of truth. But it is quite another for the reality of God on the Cross at Calvary to cause a great shock to our soul from which we never fully recover. Perhaps we do not realize until then how limited is our capacity to see in this Roman crucifixion our God suffering for us. In fact, our soul can as little bear the divine mystery of Jesus' death on a Cross as our eyes can endure gazing directly at the sun for long. The face of Jesus crucified *as our God* on a Roman Cross is quite capable of blinding us permanently. It is at the foot of the Cross that we realize we shall never fully comprehend God. Our incomprehension of God is not simply due to the infinite mystery of his divine nature. The primary incomprehension we confront comes from facing the terrible suffering he embraced as a man.

~

Anxious thought about the future is sometimes more present in religious people, and even deeply prayerful people, than in those who live for this world alone. But it is a different kind of anxiety, amounting to an unease and worry about what God may bring in the form of future trials. This concern may be contrary to a basic trust in the providential love of God. But it seems to be common enough in people who otherwise possess strong convictions of faith. Yet it should be no surprise. The Gospel makes clear that the cross awaits our life if Our Lord is sought ardently. An anticipation of unknown trials in store for us in coming days is difficult to ignore. But this knowledge is naturally limited and partial and incomplete. It is not only that any attempt at prediction about what God will permit in our lives is impossible. Such thoughts are even more misguided because none of us can place our soul in our *future* relations with God. The reality of our relations with God at a future date remains unavailable to our knowledge. All we can know is our experience already. And most people must admit that going forward in faithfulness with

God has never left them in a state of abandonment by God. On the contrary, in a recurring and mysterious way, if not always immediately, God has consistently shown that he is always close at every costly period of life. Why should that ever change? It is the quality of hope in our souls that deepens this conviction and allows us to take our thoughts from self.

~

In endless variations of milder and more desperate resemblance, the story of Job repeats itself to the present day. Job's most terrible affliction was not the loss of his loved ones, of his health, of his possessions; not the degradation of an inexplicable humiliation, reduced to scorn and contempt, with no explanation for it. The most distressful suffering was the thought he had incurred the disfavor of God while doing nothing to provoke it. With that thought arises the option to reject the very notion of God. What kind of God, without justification, can inflict retribution on innocence? It is a question that has echoed in the dark hours of many souls through many centuries. If not repudiated early on, it twists and distorts the image of God. The only proper response is not to seek an answer but, rather, to remain with no satisfying answer at all. The rush to explain God's ways by some semblance of logical analysis is foolhardy. The only answer may be to forsake an answer while offering one's faith blindly to the God who took to himself abject weakness and humiliation at Calvary.

∼

When we begin to experience the reversal of what we expect from God in embracing a religious commitment, this may be a good sign of the divine action at work. A human destiny is now starting to take shape in accord with the mystery of contradiction. Every soul seeking God in earnest is likely to find itself overcome at some point with confusion and blindness or even suffering a sense of rejection by God to some degree. The idea of a friendship with God may seem utterly impossible at such a time. The shock can be like a separation of wheat and chaff within the soul itself. To call this a purification is too easy, inasmuch as this would imply some limited duration and a conclusion to the experience. For this reversal of expectation is often not so temporary. In some contemplative lives it does not really end; rather it persists as a pattern in relations with God. Our soul over time is nonetheless capable of assimilating an important insight in this pattern. Perhaps these contradictions hide a series of questions God repeats to the souls he favors with greater love: Are you willing to carry on along dark paths with no clear direction and with silent replies? Are you ready to believe that I am still with you, never departing from you, when you have nothing at hand to confirm this but your faith? Will you accept that the shadows hide my presence? Unless we are ready to give answer to these questions, it is possible that some degree of illusion shall accompany our idea and taste of God.

~

There are disappointed contemplatives just as there are disenchanted lovers of all types. They become disillusioned at some point in their pursuit of God and, in effect, give up on the great adventure they have begun. They cross an unfortunate threshold of discouragement and stop expecting any real close- ness with God in the life of prayer. They may have once sought God with passion, but now an under- current of frustration marks their existence. How does a soul become disillusioned in love for God in this manner? This is not simply a matter of get- ting "thrown" backward by the purifications of contemplative life. The darkness inevitably expe- rienced in the contemplative encounter with God does not in itself overcome love. Some souls seem to thrive on it precisely as a goad to their love. They take the darkness as a further incentive to prove their love for their beloved. The souls who become disillusioned seem instead to allow a confused doubt to invade the initial experience of aridity and darkness in the contemplative pursuit. A pessimism enters into their spiritual life, and they never expel it. A breakdown in confidence occurs and makes them give up the deeper effort. This only reaffirms the importance of a crucial experience of poverty that begins to intensify as prayer begins to advance. Contemplative life brings an experience of darkness to the interior life, but this is not equivalent to living in a "confused" state or losing one's bearings. Not seeing does not mean we are now falling over in the dark. What keeps us protected from spiritual disappointment is the simple realization that love progresses through our self-offering. And this is of course not in imagination and sentiment, but in a dry interior act and in the overflow of generous giving of ourselves to others. There is no disappointment in souls who deepen this offering of themselves through everything. The disappointed souls, by contrast, hold on tightly to private, imaginative ideas of what a contemplative life should be.

∼

The quiet importance of supernatural hope in prayer receives too little recognition. It is a virtue of the will and affects our desire for the God who makes us poor whenever he hides from us. Hope must fortify us precisely when we experience great inner poverty because of the difficulty of God's concealment from us in prayer. At such times our desire for God can stiffen and become cramped at what seems a distant separation between our soul and God. The emptiness we taste in our desire can tempt us to an erroneous conclusion of an unbridgeable gulf between God and our soul. Hope seems to overcome this danger by infusing an assurance into the will's desire. It is as though hope and desire weld together in a yearning for God. Hope in effect saves our desire for God from a collapse that might occur if our soul focused exclusively on the experience of poverty in our desire. By means of hope, a flame will still burn even within the empty ashes of desire. We may not see or feel that flame, but it is a promise of renewed fire and further entry into the truth of the One sought.

~

Hope infuses a gritty strength of perseverance in our prayer. Despite all difficulties in seeking God and all the poverty that accompanies prayer, hope impels a steady need to keep course, never halting. No turning back from hardship, no retracting a pursuit that once begun must plunge ahead. Hesitation and irresolution are inimical to hope. On the contrary, when hope is burning in our soul, there is something analogous to the intensity of certitude the mind experiences with the increase of faith. In the case of hope, a great determination soaks into the will. It does not allow backtracking or movement in reverse. The result is that our soul's desire for God, despite every long passage through desert and dry wind, remains quietly inflamed and shows no sign of receding.

~

Unfortunately, a desire for special experiences sometimes bedevils and obsesses souls in their quest for God. It can leave them vulnerable to impressions that have no basis in objective reality. The notion of religious experience, if concentrated on inner feelings, without a real encounter beyond self, can become a form of spiritual aestheticism, a pursuit of tastes and tangible comforts, a compulsive demand for constant replenishment in the realm of inner emotion. In this distortion of true spiritual life, imagination can be a tireless companion and instigator, often inclined to interpret feelings in a grandiose manner. A narcissistic impulse easily finds a wide field for satisfaction in this search for special spiritual experiences. Illusion is hard to uncover as long as the conviction of being the recipient of special favors is upheld and defended. In contrast, more sober religious faith is necessarily opposed to this tendency because it grounds prayer in genuine faith. Faith is a personal encounter with the transcendent God, who remains in his nature beyond the tangible contact of sense or emotion. He cannot be taken hold of and enjoyed so easily. The encounter with him is more likely an experience of God's direct and difficult command while reading Jesus' harder words in the Gospel than a conviction in prayer of the touch of God laying a soft hand of solace on the hungers of one's heart.

∼

The obsessive desire for a direct experience of God often has its beginning in the mind's refusal to struggle any longer with chronic dissatisfaction in seeking God. Sometimes this giving up takes place after coming into contact with an alternative approach to spirituality that promises better results, which usually means a more tangible experience of God in prayer. It is surprising how easily prayer can be subject to a consumer's mentality. Souls are often ready to try a different method of prayer the way people are ready to try a new and improved product. When the possibility of an immediate experience of God is advertised in some semblance of bold letters, it draws some souls with great appeal. They are ready to try and try again. Some people spend years of wasted time in prayer drifting among an assortment of methods in their pursuit of experiences of God. And much of this tendency can be traced to the refusal to accept the difficult sobriety of engaging God in a dissatisfaction of mind and heart. Prayer has to be seen as a long perseverance. Otherwise, it can become an eclectic ménage of assorted practices, never stable, never facing the harder task of purification and self-emptying.

~

Mystical proclivities joined to a mind unwilling to exercise itself in the effort to know God can be a potent force for illusion in religious pursuit. And this is not so unusual. In more intensely religious people, a distrust in reason is sometimes a temptation. The use of reason is necessary in a soul's relationship with God, but this is not often attractive. Reason means hard work in the effort to know God, and usually without great satisfactions and reward. When it is abandoned to some degree, a reliance on imagination tends to replace more sober pondering and reflection. The prospect of a direct, easier road to God beckons, and for some souls the easier path is hard to refuse. The desire for shortcuts to God entices and fuels much pseudo-mysticism. The God who is slow to respond to the powers of the mind seems to offer himself much more readily to the inward realm of mystical feeling. In one sense, it is understandable that the desire to be joined in a union with God is so enticing to a soul. But there can be a narcissistic drive in this tendency. All pseudo-mysticism in one form or another is a descent into a private pursuit of God. It is marked always by an aversion to the challenge of objective criteria in the claim of experiencing God.

~

Not always is the loss of Christian faith due to an explicit rejection of doctrinal truths. Faith can be threatened also by an unreflective impulse to join foreign elements with Christian convictions. A breakdown of Christian faith is often the consequence. It is indeed a phenomenon of our time. This deterioration of traditional faith usually involves the insertion of non-Christian beliefs into one's personal understanding of Christian faith. Perhaps the initial impulse is to expand one's religious horizon. The effect, however, depending on the convictions adopted, is often to undermine and damage Christian faith. A soul ends up embracing hybrid religious formulations. The claim of being still Christian may be heard, but it is hard not to perceive the disintegration of Christian belief. In particular, the truth of the Incarnation becomes confused and compromised in its centrality. The unique reality of Jesus Christ as God and man disappears as a clear conviction. It is difficult to see, for instance, how an incorporation into a Catholic religious faith of a Hindu understanding of multiple deities or of the Buddhist absence of a personal deity can do anything less. Yet mixing religious convictions is not uncommon today. The tendency to careless and incautious inclusiveness in religious commitments is taken by some people as a sign of sophistication in the personal approach to religion. Some people seem to make the co-existence within their own soul of disparate beliefs the goal of their religious striving. But the result is more than likely a tragic disappearance of traditional Christian faith.

∼

The notion of religious experience does have an inherent ambiguity. It can refer to the ordinary life of faith, the personal engagement with the unseen and invisible, the normal life of prayer for the religious believer. Or it can mean some claim of a special experience of God in the realm of the mystical, something with tangible effects that goes beyond the usual religious experience rooted in faith. The personal conviction of an encounter with transcendent reality, with God, is shared by both. In either case, this is a formidable claim. When it extends in the second instance to an assertion of some tangible contact with God, it is capable, surely, of error and exaggeration. For that reason, the second claim draws at times a skeptical reaction. And yet the declaration of an immediate encounter with God himself is precisely the testimony of Christian revelation in pronouncing Jesus of Nazareth to be God in the flesh. In one sense, all spiritual desire must be directed to a real encounter with God incarnate in the flesh. The presence of the Eucharist offered in sacrifice at Mass or in a tabernacle is a constant return to this mystery of real encounter with God in the flesh. The Eucharist allows a personal meeting with Jesus Christ, though of course this is not confirmed by any extraordinary experience of the senses. It is lived in faith, and faith itself provides the firm assurance of being in the presence of the Almighty One concealed in the Host. For most people, even very holy people, this is enough. They ask no more, and need no more, because they possess all they desire in kneeling before him. Their own "mystical" life, it might be said, is fully satisfied by ordinary contact with the reality unseen to them. They need no visions or spoken words to enhance their real religious experience of Our Lord present before their blind eyes.

13

Contemplative Aftereffects

"Now I occupy my soul and all my energy in His service; I no longer tend the herd, nor have I any other work now that my every act is love."

—Saint John of the Cross

"Christianity wishes to intensify passion to its highest pitch."

—Søren Kierkegaard

"The more recollected the person lives in his innermost soul, the greater the power he radiates outward and the greater the influence he exerts on others."

—Saint Edith Stein

The life of prayer will always overflow the time of prayer. This is especially true when the prayer is contemplative. The hunger of the soul extends beyond prayer itself and is carried into the hours of the day. Again, the personal experience of this may vary among souls. But the principle in itself is indisputable. A contemplative effort must be exercised to become more sensitive to the manner in which

our soul is drawn to live out a contemplative hunger for
God beyond the time of prayer. The contemplative life
is not a matter of simply waiting for a return to prayer;
rather, it is an expression of the fullness of a life. It finds
its support and sustenance in a self-giving outside prayer
that has been stirred initially in the time of prayer. The
generosity of soul we exercise outside of prayer is in turn
a way to enhance our soul's love for God when we return
to prayer.

Quickly and even noticeably, contemplative prayer
intensifies a desire for the presence of God *outside*
the time of prayer. The effect is detected primarily
in one's vision. After the attraction of God's silent
love in prayer, it is strangely our eyes that are most
affected. They carry a lingering hunger for an encounter with God into the observations of the day.
The hunger is like a low, subdued flame burning
beneath the impressions that meet our eyes, waiting for a deeper recognition. Soon we discover that
God is hiding signs of his presence in ordinary moments. The result is that our eyes begin to search
differently in a day, anxious for contact with God.
They tend more often to notice God's interventions, the inexplicable timing of chance encounters. They pierce through veil and external veneer
to the quiet invitations contained in the hour at
hand. Even a small awareness of a gesture of God
provokes a yearning that does not release the soul.
These recognitions begin to affect prayer itself, for

we carry a more intense longing for God back to silent prayer. A rhythm of seeking God ensues, a rhythm in and out of prayer. Our soul's longing for God in a chapel stretches into a yearning for him outside prayer. The discovery of God's presence outside prayer stokes in turn a flame of love for him that is brought back to prayer. The encounter with him outside prayer provides an easier access to his real presence in the time of silent prayer.

∼

There may be no continuing grace of contemplation in prayer unless we learn to embrace a different form of seeing and attentiveness to reality. Our longing for a hidden God depends much on a receptive attraction toward all that exists. A concealed beauty permeates all reality, and we must search for it, even if it cannot be perceived at all times. But it is present and requires an attentiveness of love on our part if it is to be seen at all. Likewise, there is a beauty of hiddenness in the mystery of God encountered in deeper prayer. The discovery of this concealed beauty depends in part on the discovery of a depth of silence at the heart of reality. We must seek the silent truth of real things, with a gaze of longing in the eye and spirit, if we are to be more open and receptive to God dwelling in the hidden silence of our soul during an hour of prayer.

~

A certain lack of attention in the interior life—the failure to turn toward a recognition of God's presence—this omission perhaps undermines at times the favorable beginnings in many contemplative lives. Without a steady hunger to attend to an obscure recognition of God's presence outside of silent prayer, our soul will soon find more difficulty in the encounter with his concealed presence during quiet prayer. We are more likely to receive contemplative graces when an interior thirst for God begins to consume all moments in our life, including the least "contemplative" activities. The search for the sign of his providential action in the unlikely hour and place may be one essential factor determining the continued growth in contemplative grace. This is not an imaginative game, as though by our own volition we can bring God into our day. It is a spiritual alertness to perceive that he is there already. This recognition has the effect of removing chance and coincidence from the encounters that flow through a day and replacing them with the deeper awareness of God's providence at work.

~

Every soul comes to possess a unique spiritual character for better or for worse depending on the quality of faith in it. It is a question, not just of faith, but how faith is lived. Faith is not simply an acceptance of doctrinal truth. After a certain point, faith is sensitivity to the immediate presence of God in daily life. Either we learn to be receptive to the mystery of God and come to know more over time the interventions of God at unexpected hours, his requests and invitations arriving in a manner impossible to predict, or we resist this possibility and consider God detached from our small life. By that refusal, we carve jagged edges into our spirit. We are unable to imagine God so near to our lives. We will never come to know that he is trying to surprise us, prodding our flesh and our thoughts in the midst of mundane routines in order to draw our recognition.

∿

A prayer of gratitude will always influence our perceptions outside prayer. Once we are in the habit of thanking God for *all* that is happening in our life, including the harder challenges, a new realization awakens. The providential nature of events begins to show itself more. We "see" the hand of God more at work or at least trust implicitly that his reasons will show themselves in time. The actual presence of a divine request in a day's circumstances becomes more available to our attention. The sense of spiritual opportunity increases, the sense that God is giving us a chance to prove our love in still another way. All these effects are due

to a conscious effort to express gratitude to God
for all he is doing.

~

Every inexhaustible truth of God that stretches beyond our comprehension in prayer can benefit our
lives outside prayer—although this may be a benefit not entirely practical in its blessing. We might,
for instance, ponder in prayer the immense love
of God for the poorest people, yet without really
penetrating beyond the surface of this truth. The
effort may yield hardly more than an abstraction
in our mind, and we may only lurch and stumble
in the direction of its truth. Afterward, however,
the same truth is likely to linger quietly in our
mind and affect our perception of a day's realities.
The more profane affairs of a day do not draw our
usual preoccupation and focus so strongly. To take
up worldly thoughts or get caught up in business
dealings can be very unattractive. It is as though
the truth of God's love for the poor and the abandoned, wrestled with earlier yet not grasped adequately, still provokes hunger in our soul and
prevents an exclusive concentration on worldly
concerns. It is not that our mind after prayer will
tolerate only a gaze on beautiful thoughts and infinite vistas. Rather, it may be that the prior reflection in prayer on a truth of God's love for the
poor introduces a craving that does not disappear

and that our soul then carries into the common encounters of a day. This effect of prayer may not be entirely beneficial to the accomplishment of all the practical tasks we face in the day. But in this example at least it may be a wonderful aid to the discovery of God's love for the most neglected persons around us.

~

The experience of prayer lingering as an influence upon a day's reality is not surprising. It should not be thought a rejection of the mundane and commonplace, as though we accepted to live only on an elevated plane of pristine detachment, separated from the harder demands of human life. The effect is simply to pierce our awareness with a sense of division between the significant and enduring in contrast to that which is quickly passing away. A sharper sense of God's providence enters into the flow of a day. This awareness of God's unseen presence is perhaps a compensation for our mind's inability to gain entry into God's mystery during an earlier reflection in prayer. In contrast to the frustration of understanding little during prayer, the tasks we take up in a day can be permeated with a sense of purpose that our earlier thought did not find in thinking about God. Surely the reason for this clarity outside prayer is the hidden presence of God affecting our vision. Not that our perception changes in any dramatic manner. It is simply that our soul carries a hunger it would not possess except for its earlier searching in silent prayer. This hunger becomes part of our encounter with every reality we face in a day. After the earlier incomprehension experienced in prayer, God now seems to blind us in a different manner. Our mind is unable to give itself to the false veneer of the passing elements in temporal realities. Instead, God pierces us with a different, hardly noticed desire to know in some inexplicable manner the concealed presence of eternity hiding in the current hour.

~

Providing explanations is not a special talent of prayerful people. They may be proficient in skills of analysis and persuasion only as much as any other man or woman. And yet they often seem to recognize, by an intuitive penetration of love, and far more keenly, what is truthful and real than someone capable by native intelligence of sharp scrutiny and insight. Their knowledge of reality comes from a wisdom of love, not simply from natural intelligence. What they are unable to articulate at times, they grasp through a sensitivity rooted in their contemplative love. A quality of attentiveness inseparable from their love would seem to explain this. This concentration of attention in holy, contem-

plative people is not due to an act of will. Nor is it
comparable to the absorption of a mind in a subject of interest. It is simply the symptom of a soul
alive with desire and love. This attentiveness flow-
ing from love is the source of their deeper, more
penetrating awareness. Under the influence of love,
their mind is never engaged only in a solitary exercise of thought. Rather, it is oriented outward by
love to realities beyond self, drawn by an inclination to love truth wherever it is found. Whether
that other reality is a person or the immediate event
at hand, contemplative souls seem to absorb themselves in this real otherness beyond self. It is the
source of their deeper, more accurate penetration
into truth. But it is also an exercise that we can
learn to practice. And, indeed, it is an essential effort if we are to become more contemplative in
our own lives.

～

The great souls respond to immediate recognitions that may have no prior warning or preparation behind them. Their generosity of soul already makes them ready and eager for the acts that
flow out of them. When the chance to give suddenly faces them, they do not hesitate. They are
not so caught and bound by private concerns and
self-preoccupation. They do not have to ruminate
and discern when the divine request is suddenly

upon them. They rather leap to the demand of the moment that newly presents itself. The response of Maximilian Kolbe suggests this kind of spontaneous act. There was likely no concrete preparation for the heroic offer he made to replace a father facing a vindictive death sentence in Auschwitz, and yet a strong, decisive act took place. A leap out of the privacy of his love for God to the need of another is the only adequate explanation for the spontaneity of such an act.

~

"Men like certainty" (Blaise Pascal). The satisfaction of knowing anything with some degree of assurance makes our relations with God inherently difficult. And so we tend to avoid the troubling thought that we may not know enough of God or what God is really asking of us. We may prefer not to engage this uncertainty and perhaps give up too easily, treating God's desires as unknowable. We replace the search for God's more personal request to us with a goal only of good behavior, which is assumed to be all we can know of his will. But this limited approach cannot take us very far in relations with God. It is a sign of a lack of deeper prayer. The request to God to know his will is surely not refused if we pray earnestly for that knowledge. He finds his way to answer. If we ask how he does so, the answer may come in prayer. Often, however, it comes not in prayer but in surprising words from people we did not expect to meet, in coincidental encounters that speak quietly of God's preference for a choice he wants from us. And then it is not good to insist on a second sign; but rather, it is best to remain poor, accepting that God has spoken sufficiently. He wants us to trust in his providential ways of hiddenness and not revert to our own demands for certainty and sure proof.

~

When we feel compelled to overcome difficulties quickly by some mode of efficiency, we should realize that this need is contrary to a deeper contemplative spirit. That is not to say we should not struggle in an active manner when facing problems. But pragmatic solutions often become an excuse for aggressive choices focused solely on achieving results. A reliance on ourselves commonly drives this tendency, usually without taking the trouble to pray. There is a cost, naturally, in triumphs achieved through an exercise of our willfulness and without recourse to God. We may win victories, even draw public notice for our capable nature, and yet miss what God was asking us to experience in facing some difficulty. A divine request goes unheard and is overlooked because we lack the patience to observe a spiritual invitation more closely. Many difficulties we face are meant to expose our poverty or to perceive with greater love the poverty of another soul. We must bring this poverty back with us to the time of prayer. On the other hand, we are not likely to learn much about real poverty while enjoying a steady proficiency in solving problems by our own capable nature. We might consider, too, that not all our most efficient solutions are blessed by God.

~

The spirit of sacrifice is always present in contemplative life. It is an overflow of the yearning to love and to give ourselves for others. At the same time, sacrifice in contemplative life displays a distinct character in that it is never "self-perfective" in purpose. The motive for sacrificial choices in contemplative life can never be an improvement of ourselves. Sacrifice is a genuine contemplative principle only when it turns our attention away from self. In this sense, it parallels the common effect of contemplative prayer, which likewise leads to a diminished attention cast upon self. Either sacrifice makes us forget ourselves, or it is not worth the trouble. If the cost entailed in sacrifice should begin instead to consume our thought and lead to excessive concern with deprivations, this would contradict the essential reason for undertaking any sacrifice. In that sense, the experience of any hardship or pain that accompanies sacrifice can be an obstacle to it. This can quickly make a caricature of sacrifice and produce the opposite effect of what should take place in sacrifice. If we attend too fixedly on the cost of a sacrifice, or, for that matter, on the benefits expected from it, we end by being taken up solely with ourselves in what amounts to another self-centered form of activity. Only in giving for the good of another, in directing our action for an intention beyond self, can any self-denial or sacrifice be a fruitful spiritual pursuit. This inclination is precisely a fruit of a deeper offering of ourselves to God in prayer.

∽

Sacrifice in contemplative life does not as such find its rationale in the correction of flaws or in the strengthening of our moral fiber. It is not for the purpose of building character or reinforcing areas of our life that need some greater discipline. Sacrifice in its genuine contemplative form has one sure sign of value: that without any direct effort to do so, it leads to a release from self. In this regard, it has the same orientation as love and all deeper prayer. It is no coincidence that the spirit of sacrifice thrives in an intense contemplative manner only when sacrifice is moved by love for someone.

It is only in a time of love that sacrifice is fully alive and energetic. The deeper a love for another person, the more the inclination is present to sacrifice. It is an infallible symptom of greater love.

～

There is another subtle and striking dimension to this link of love and sacrifice. The most intense sacrificial actions are at times provoked by the experience of a deprivation in the experience of love. The desire for sacrifice may burn most intensely in those times when our soul knows its own lack of love, its insufficient love, usually during our prayer. When the desire to love is strongly felt and yet is unsatisfied, sacrifice for the beloved is the only option. The drive to sacrifice is inflamed precisely when the loved one is absent or inaccessible in some manner. The separation from the presence of a beloved, the delay in meeting again, the long wait for the beloved, even the silence of the loved one when present—all of these provoke a desire to strip and empty self, to make the self disappear, to experience a vanquishing of self in some permanent manner. Considering the nature of God's concealment from the souls he loves, this is surely a reason why those who love him most are always more sacrificial in their lives.

～

The possibility exists that much good that we may do for others is at the time of its performance hidden from our awareness. We are ignorant of a deeper significance in these actions. We do not know the influence we are leaving behind, and no doubt it is better that way. But it is also necessary to consider this possibility, if we are to bear fruit for souls. The awareness refines and concentrates our motivations. By exercising a pure intention to do good for another, focused solely on a benefit to the other and not on what we might receive, we may affect another soul in a lasting spiritual way that we will never know. The implicit desire to "touch the soul" of another person by our action surely contributes to this effect. Religious influence is a subtle, concealed phenomenon. The effect of one soul on another is usually recognized only later by the one who has been influenced. In one sense, the hiddenness of these influences has an analogy to the writings of an author who has taken his conscious thought in a definite direction while not realizing his greater and more original inspiration is contained in a concealed intuition he has not understood or noticed. But it is nevertheless present and effective and unmistakable. The life of prayer must direct us in a more concentrated manner to this desire to reach the souls of others. Deeper prayer will always pierce our soul with a desire to bring souls to God.

14

Observations in Brief

"When Jesus takes you into himself to give you to souls, wherever you go means a life of isolation. We find that apparent contradiction in Christ, a hidden, contemplative soul who ended up giving himself to men, allowing himself to be consumed by them."

—Charles de Foucauld

"All things hide a mystery; all things are veils hiding God."

—Blaise Pascal

"We have heard the fact, let us seek the mystery."

—Saint Augustine

Some last thoughts on contemplative life converge on the question of fruitfulness. The contemplative life is directed toward the spiritual benefit of others, or else it does not persist. In one sense, this must be a conscious intention, maintained throughout a lifetime of prayer and sacrificial self-giving. Yet in any true contemplative life, it is not a difficult choice to be drawn to offer prayer for others. The contemplative life finds its essential purpose in a tenacious offering for others. But precisely this aspect of a life lived for others who are in many cases never seen or encountered requires faith in a more intense degree. The offering for others of a contemplative soul is deprived of the tangible satisfaction that, for example, works of charity for the poor might have. Consequently, the contemplative's offering must reach down into a deep layer of faith. If there is an indisputable truth that can be said of them, the true contemplatives are souls of a very pronounced faith. It is perhaps their primary distinction that their faith in turn makes them, even in their hiddenness, great souls of love.

If a contemplative life is to advance in love, it can have no boundaries that limit and enclose it, no barricades behind which love might be tended in a careful cultivation. A contemplative love that seeks only the familiar garden dries up. Contemplative life in one sense demands a breaking free from confinement and every narrow generosity. It thrives in extending itself beyond the walls of enclosure in an offering of love for souls that are many and still unknown. It flourishes, even in a cloister or monastery, only when the heart and soul are missionary and seek forgotten souls most in danger of being lost.

∼

"Are we ready and willing to offer everything to God?" The question will trail and pursue lives that

have indeed made a great offering to God, inter-
rupting at intervals and bringing back to mind what
may be a buried recognition. These are lives that at
some point offer themselves to God with an unreserved generosity, in disregard of all consequence,
ready in that blind hour for all that might come. But
does the offering of that day continue and deepen
over time? Or at some juncture in life does a soul
step back and reconsider, negotiating for a revi-
sion of the words of offering, replacing the "everything" it once offered with a more modest pro-
posal? Is this stepping back and this preference for
the partial what Raïssa Maritain meant when writing in her journal that our generosity can become
in time a "dead offering"? The only answer must
be to renew and deepen the full gift of ourselves
to God.

~

How does our soul arrive, once again, at the threshold of discovering anew and more deeply a religious
truth? How do we experience again, for instance,
the spiritual beauty of offering ourselves in prayer
that may have become gradually obscured under a
veil of shadow and hard strain? Perhaps this happens only after a silent waiting mixed with longing, anticipating nothing in image or thought, but
nonetheless entering into an expectancy for a truth
that must come from beyond our soul. Afterward,
when an understanding is received that we must

again offer our lives fully to God, even without a clear thought or words to help us, we may realize that this insight of a need to offer ourselves was slowly emerging as though from shadows precisely during the time of patient silence and waiting.

~

In endless variations, contemplative life means living in proximity to the sacredness of God's hidden presence. But it is the discovery as well that his closeness offers no steady or reliable or predictable satisfactions. Rather, the truth of the divine presence includes a refusal to be held and possessed even by those who love him most. Perhaps a definitive threshold of contemplative life is crossed when a soul finds no defeat, no real loss, in this lack of possession, no lasting frustration, but strangely an answer in poverty to the deeper longing until then buried within it. For it finds precisely in a perpetual yearning for God the encounter it prefers to any possession. It would not exchange this longing for any temporary satisfaction. The longing for God, when it is vibrant and strong, leads us inevitably to pray for souls in great need.

~

Only in poverty do we intensify a real confidence in God. Those who become truly poor in spirit no longer chase after external signs that would confirm the status of their relations with God. They surmount that insecurity. They no longer seek to possess a clear knowledge of this sort. They live instead in deeper hope, in the certitude of hope, without any need to have signs. They have crossed a threshold of trust in poverty itself, with all its obscure and indecipherable contradictions, as the only path to God. The God of the poor is now their beloved, a God who arouses great confidence in our personal offering for souls precisely when our own soul tastes greater emptiness in itself.

∼

In a certain manner, it is the task of contemplative life to gaze courageously into the silence of the night, sometimes the dry, windless, barren night, and yet refuse to be intimidated. When the night is for the moment all the soul has, it ought to seek no more favorable time for meeting God. When accepted and welcomed, the night itself becomes the path of pilgrimage toward his unseen light. Sometimes these nights are long and seem endless, but in a true contemplative life there is no stopping, no halting, no rest sought even in the strained hours. Yet some nights are different, as every contemplative soul knows, when one's offering for others has vivid clarity, and these nights bring a contentment like the shine of a full moon on an open field.

～

In prayer, to take the leap into the silence and remain there, without seeking to find security in words—this is much harder than we think. The effort, however, is worth the trouble, for it requires that we listen in that silence, listen with attention, waiting for a presence of someone other than ourselves to emerge again from this silence. And often the whisper heard in that silence of our soul is the renewed request to offer ourselves for souls.

～

For some people, the intensity of their belief in God is matched by an inclination to ask questions of God. The correlation is not a sign of disrespect or of doubt. They would not ask questions in this manner except for a conviction that God can be addressed in an utterly personal manner. In fact, their questions, which often begin with a "why is it" or "how can it be", tend to summon a deeper act of faith from their souls. Inasmuch as their questions are not answered so readily, as usually they are not, these questions plunge their souls much more blindly into the mystery of God. The unanswered question demands a surrender to God and a greater offering. The surrender can only be made with a conviction that God has heard the request for some light and accepted the offering of one's soul for others. If no clarity is forthcoming, the soul can still remain at peace, certain that God has been listening and will extend grace to others.

~

Logical labors of thought that seem to provide clear answers and explanations are usually false solutions in the realm of sacred mystery. Only in waiting and in darkness do quiet spiritual insights come upon us, and when they do so, they are like the light slowly emerging at dawn. And often they have to do with our need to offer ourselves more fully in love for others.

~

We must ask often for the grace to experience the true impotence of all our own spiritual efforts without the help of God. It is not a request that comes quickly to our mind. Yet it is crucial to realize this truth of our own autonomous incapacity for spiritual fruitfulness and to experience it. Work for God is too easily considered by a standard of achievement in the world. But there are no real successes in any spiritual work that are equivalent to an accomplishment in the world. Certain patterns, however, begin to show after a time. A work desired by God seems always to include some measure of frustration and failed exertion. At the same time, failure in a work undertaken for God often conceals fruits whose delay in manifesting themselves is only temporary. It is hard to accept these patterns until they are observed over a certain length of time in our lives. Nothing significant is ever done for God and for souls without some taste of crucifixion and the offering it requires from us.

~

Truthfulness, if relentless, that digging closer to the center, is always feared by some. And yet it is a necessity without which no contemplative life has ever been lived. On the other hand, those who seek to accommodate themselves to others, to conform to the prevailing opinions, who determine their thought with a careful eye on their companions, who pursue communal agreement as an especially esteemed value, these people may live comfortably with their convictions. Yet surely their souls are closed off from the challenges of God that lead to deeper prayer. They are deaf to the spirit of contradiction that God inevitably demands of a soul of deeper prayer. No one who claims fidelity to God will escape a need to draw away sometimes from easy companionship with the crowd. We must be alone at times, or else we will join with others in compromising spiritual values—thereby losing our true life, not offering what we must for the sake of love.

~

Can we offer ourselves to the "all" that God is currently asking of us? The question rises up quietly in prayer, and if we listen carefully, we perceive that this question does not disappear but is present to some degree always in our prayer. The act of self-oblation is never finished, never completed, and so the question remains, returning to our prayer, taking up a permanent corner, as it were, in the silence of our soul. The presence of this question does not make a great drama of every hour of prayer. On the contrary, the "all" that God asks us to offer may at times concern simply our possessive impulse to retain a minor attachment or to protect our own importance. By our accessibility to the ordinary requests, however, and especially those that make us a servant to another's need, we become available to new and greater demands that will extend our love farther over time toward a more complete immolation.

~

The most telling evidence of our need to grow in love may be our omissions when an opportunity for a smaller gesture of love presents itself. Lack of generosity in the small moments of a day can have a cumulative effect on our soul. The danger is that we begin to lose awareness of the *indistinguishable* nature of love's demands. God does not measure differences in love according to the apparent magnitude of what we choose in that moment. Nor does he compare one hour to the next when he asks us to give ourselves in love in the present hour. For God, all that matters is our willingness to give fully in love to the current hour of need no matter what is available for our choosing.

～

The vast separation between the good life and the holy life is always far more than we realize. The difference is not evident simply in the exterior activity of a life. The generous accomplishments of a good person may outshine the limited works of the holy person. What distinguishes the holy person is the interior quality of a soul seeking God, and this is often not seen so visibly. The good life will always be observable to some degree, but whether or not a life is truly holy can easily be concealed in its essential truth. The most important acts of a holy life take place in secret, within quiet depths of the soul. And these most important acts are the offerings it makes for others. There is no great love of

God unless a soul is great in offering itself for others. And this begins in the intensity of its prayer, where God alone sees.

~

The word holiness ought not to be tossed about too lightly, as though the reality were easily reached. There is a danger that an overworked and casual evocation of holiness as the goal of life reduces the immense challenge of giving all to God to a manageable habit of steady, low-cost generosities. Dorothy Day kept on her bedside table a striking phrase of Dostoevsky that conveys, by contrast, the starker reality of a true offering: "Love in action is a harsh and dreadful thing compared to love in dreams." It is precisely the harsh and dreadful nature of sacrificial love that makes such love and the offering that accompanies it most fruitful for the salvation of souls.

~

There may be a wisdom in the usual preference of contemplatives for living behind closed walls. For one thing, it protects them in their desire for self-effacement and disappearance from view. The contemplatives who remain in the world do not seem to enjoy this protection. Yet those who forego the cloistered walls are likely to find that their soul's hiddenness is maintained without great difficulty.

They do not have to devise stratagems for concealment. It is always the case that the secret truth of contemplatives is largely unknown to others around them. In fact, this may be as true in monasteries as in the world. The beauty of this contemplative inclination in the eyes of God may be that their offering for others is precisely a hidden secret.

~

We should not analyze the interior experience of silent prayer too much. At the same time, an examination of our attitude toward prayer is occasionally necessary. It is possible for us to allow our prayer to become primarily an obligation rather than a real attraction. When prayer is a task to be completed, another work to finish, the effect is a gradual tightening of the heart in coldness. We cannot expect a personal relationship with God if we perceive prayer as a burden. Prayer as the fulfillment of duty will leave us outside the door, in the servant's quarters. Only prayer returned to over and over as a great passion in search of the Lord's personal presence and as an offering for others will grant mysterious access to silent communications from God to our soul.

~

On certain days when prayer seems harder, we must dive inward in the direction of our own nothingness in order to arrive at a true spirit of adoration in prayer. The prayer of adoration and the realization of our own nothingness are interdependent. One without the other can be false, lacking its essential counterpart. It may be only after much struggle with our own insignificance and nothingness that our soul truly learns how to adore God in a pure manner and, thereafter, to love other souls with a purer intention.

∼

A task in prayer that must be repeated with regularity: to search for the deeper solitary region of the heart where a single word spoken in silence has more impact on our soul than hours of replete eloquence taking place at the shallows of life.

∼

Contemplative life compels at times a great, pressing need for a self-offering in prayer that must be made without inner strength or courage, without a clear reason for the urgency of this act, without a promise even of being heard, but in the sheer conviction that to offer our soul entirely to God is the only way at the present hour to avoid collapsing in our perseverance.

~

After a while, we cannot draw closer to divine love without an equally strong desire to draw others to the gift of divine mercy. Failing that, our soul will forsake a grace that is meant henceforth to give our life its primary spiritual intensity. Earlier this may not be recognized, but after a certain juncture, we must be dominated by the desire for divine goodness to become manifest to others. Otherwise, much of our spiritual pursuit can be simply vanity and self-seeking.

~

No doubt the saints prayed much more for the glory of God to be made manifest to others than for any personal experience they might enjoy of God. They were intent that God become known by others, that his goodness be observed and his merciful love be recognized. They understood God to be inviting souls everywhere, to be bending over souls in need. They were close to God, and most of the time they knew surely that he was accompanying their lives. Nonetheless, their own experience of God was secondary to the more essential truth of God's desire for the salvation of souls.

～

We have to accustom ourselves more in faith to the fact that God sometimes prepares us over a long stretch of time for a single lengthy minute when he will show his crucified face in the concrete misery of a poor man's lonely pain. This is precisely a contemplative recognition, and it is not available simply by reason of our proximity to the lives of the poor. What awaits a contemplative soul who remains living in the world are these new encounters with the Passion of Christ once again mysteriously exposed to the eyes of the soul.

～

Faith in a crucified God who accepted to bear immense malice while keeping silent may be the only answer to inexplicable evil and human suffering. And yet it is an answer we should not suggest too quickly to souls whose agony is accentuated by a sense of distance from God in their present hour of affliction. The unsatisfactory nature of this answer may reside simply in the fact of speaking at all. No *words* about Jesus' silence during the Passion are suitable. The answer to suffering is in the mystery of the silence itself that Jesus displayed on the Cross. The soul in suffering has to enter this silence and the prayer of offering that accompanied it in order to hear this divine answer. Then possibly it is heard.

~

If prayer advances, it is because the soul becomes less capable of praying without divine help. All must be received, all must be spurred by another, even the desire to go to prayer. In the hours of prayer, one primary need recurs continually. Our soul must place its hand out like a beggar in supplication and then wait. We must let go of all else we would seek to grasp and all that we might be tempted to lift up to God as a gift of our own. Nothing belongs exclusively to our own soul; all must be offered. To acknowledge this lack of possession is difficult. But the release of everything that might be claimed for self is an essential condition for any deeper contemplative prayer.

~

It must be recalled at times that in prayer we live off alms from unknown benefactors. Certainly others are praying for us, offering for us, whenever we find ourselves attracted to prayer. Even more deeply, we are the recipients of a mysterious benefaction when prayer becomes a passion in our life. The poorer we become in ourselves due to this passion for God, the more we may draw the prayers

of the saints in heaven and of the Virgin Mary herself, who know that this poverty can lead in time
to the making of greater offerings by a soul. We
ought to pray for this grace of a great passion for
God.

~

"It is always dangerous to be half Christian."

—Jacques Maritain